ZIG MASTERY PROFESSIONALS

PROFESSIONALS

Build High-Performance Systems

BENJAMIN SAMUEL

TABLE OF CONTENT

PREFACE

In the ever-evolving landscape of software development, a constant tension exists between performance, safety, and developer experience. For too long, achieving excellence in one often meant compromising on another. High-performance languages frequently demanded meticulous manual memory management, leading to potential pitfalls and increased development complexity. Safer languages sometimes introduced runtime overhead that hindered performance-critical applications.

Enter Zig: a language meticulously crafted to bridge this divide. Zig is not merely another programming language; it represents a thoughtful and pragmatic approach to building robust, high-performance software without sacrificing safety or developer sanity. It empowers you to wield low-level control when necessary, offering fine-grained management of memory and hardware, while simultaneously providing powerful abstractions and compile-time safety guarantees.

This book is your comprehensive guide to harnessing the power of Zig. We will embark on a journey that begins with the fundamentals of the language, exploring its unique syntax, powerful type system, and innovative features like error unions and comptime execution. We will then delve into the practical application of Zig across diverse domains, from crafting efficient system utilities and building high-performance networked applications to leveraging its strengths in concurrency, metaprogramming, and even WebAssembly.

Throughout this exploration, we will emphasize not just *how* to write Zig code, but also *how* to write it effectively. We will examine best practices for memory management, error handling, concurrency, and optimization, equipping you with the knowledge to build reliable and performant software. We will also delve into Zig's exceptional C interoperability, a cornerstone of its pragmatic design, allowing you to seamlessly leverage the vast ecosystem of existing C libraries.

This book is for developers of all backgrounds who are seeking a language that offers a compelling alternative to the traditional performance-versus-safety trade-off. Whether you are a seasoned systems programmer looking for a safer and more modern toolchain, a game developer striving for maximum performance, a web developer exploring the potential of high-performance WebAssembly, or simply a curious mind eager to explore the next generation of programming languages, this book will provide you with the knowledge and practical skills to unlock the potential of Zig.

Prepare to discover a language that empowers you to build the future of software – software that is fast, safe, and a joy to create. Welcome to the world of Zig.

CHAPTER 1

Embracing the Zig Philosophy: A Professional's Perspective

1.1 The Case for Zig: Addressing Modern Software Challenges

Let's delve deeper into "The Case for Zig: Addressing Modern Software Challenges".

Modern software development faces a complex landscape of increasing demands. Applications need to be faster, more reliable, more secure, and often need to interact with a plethora of existing systems. Traditional languages, while powerful, sometimes fall short in addressing these challenges holistically. Zig emerges as a contender aiming to provide a better balance, particularly in the realm of systems programming and performance-critical applications.[1]

Here's a more granular look at the modern software challenges Zig seeks to address:

1. The Growing Burden of Complexity:

Problem: Software projects are becoming increasingly large and intricate.[2] This complexity manifests in sprawling codebases, intricate build systems, and a web of dependencies.[3] Languages with features like implicit conversions, complex object-oriented hierarchies, and intricate macro systems can obscure the underlying mechanics, making code harder to understand, debug, and maintain. Developers spend more time deciphering existing code and less time building new features.

Zig's Approach: Zig champions **simplicity and explicitness**. Its syntax is deliberately minimal, reducing the number of ways to achieve the same result.[4] There are no hidden control flows like exceptions or implicit memory allocations happening behind the scenes.[5] This design philosophy aims to make the behavior of Zig code more predictable and easier to reason about.[6] When you read Zig code, what you see is what you get.

Example: Consider a scenario where you need to handle a potential error. In some languages, an exception might be thrown and caught far away from the point of failure, making it harder to trace the error's origin. In Zig, error handling is explicit using error unions.[7] You must explicitly check for and handle potential errors at the call site.

Code snippet

```
const std = @import("std");
const fs = std.fs;

pub fn readFile(path: []const u8) ![]u8 {
    const file = try fs.openFile(path, .{}) catch |err| return err;
    defer file.close();
                        const        contents        =        try
file.readToEndAlloc(std.heap.page_allocator);
    return contents;
}

pub fn main() !void {
    const result = readFile("my_file.txt");
    if (result) |contents| {
        std.debug.print("File contents: {}\n", .{contents});
        std.heap.page_allocator.free(contents);
```

```
  } else |err| {
    std.debug.print("Error reading file: {}\n", .{err});
  }
}
```

In this example, the `!` in the function signature indicates that `readFile` can return an error. The caller (`main` function) must explicitly handle this potential error using an `if (result) |contents| else |err|` block. This explicitness makes error handling more visible and less prone to being overlooked.

2. The Persistent Challenge of Safety and Reliability:

Problem: Memory safety issues (like buffer overflows, use-after-free, and dangling pointers) and concurrency bugs continue to plague software systems, leading to crashes, security vulnerabilities, and unpredictable behavior. Languages like C and C++, while offering fine-grained control, place a significant burden on the developer to manage memory correctly and handle concurrency safely.[8]

Zig's Approach: Zig aims for **safety without sacrificing performance**.[9] While it provides manual memory management, it incorporates features to help developers avoid common pitfalls:

No Implicit Memory Allocation: Unlike some higher-level languages, Zig doesn't have hidden memory allocations happening behind the scenes in regular control flow or function calls.[10] This makes memory usage more predictable.

Optional Types: The ?T syntax forces developers to explicitly consider the possibility of a value being absent (null-like), reducing null pointer exceptions.[11]

Error Handling as Part of the Type System: As seen in the previous example, error handling is integrated into the type system, making it harder to ignore potential failures.

Built-in Testing with Memory Safety Checks: Zig's testing framework includes checks for memory leaks and other memory-related issues.[12]

Comptime: Zig's compile-time execution capability allows for certain checks and computations to be performed at compile time, catching potential errors before runtime.

Example (Optional Types):

Code snippet

```
const std = @import("std");

fn findUserById(id: u32) ?User {
    // Simulate finding a user; might return null if not found
    if (id == 123) {
        return User{ .id = 123, .name = "Alice" };
    } else {
        return null;
    }
}
```

```
pub fn main() !void {
    const user1 = findUserById(123);
    if (user1) |u| {
        std.debug.print("Found user: {}\n", .{u.name});
    } else {
        std.debug.print("User not found.\n", .{});
    }

    const user2 = findUserById(456);
    if (user2) |u| {
        std.debug.print("Found user: {}\n", .{u.name});
    } else {
        std.debug.print("User not found.\n", .{});
    }
}

const User = struct {
    id: u32,
    name: []const u8,
};
```

Here, ?User indicates that findUserById might return either a User struct or null. The if (user) construct forces the developer to explicitly handle both cases, preventing potential errors if user is null.

3. The Ever-Present Demand for Performance and Efficiency:

Problem: Many modern applications, especially in areas like game development, high-frequency trading, embedded systems, and operating systems, have stringent performance requirements. The overhead introduced by garbage collection, virtual machines, or complex runtime environments in some languages can be a significant bottleneck.

Zig's Approach: Zig is designed for **high performance from the ground up**.[13] Its manual memory management gives developers precise control over memory layout and allocation, crucial for optimization.[14] The lack of a large runtime environment means less overhead and more direct interaction with the underlying hardware. Zig also supports features that enable low-level optimizations, such as SIMD (Single Instruction, Multiple Data) through compiler intrinsics.[15]

Example (Illustrative - Low-level optimization often involves more complex code): While a simple example might not fully showcase the performance benefits, consider the directness of memory allocation:

Code snippet

```
const std = @import("std");

pub fn main() !void {
    // Allocate an array of 10 integers on the heap
    const array = try std.heap.page_allocator.alloc(i32, 10);
    defer std.heap.page_allocator.free(array);

    for (0..10) |i| {
        array[i] = @intCast(i32, i * 2);
    }
```

```
    std.debug.print("{any}\n", .{array});
}
```

Here, the allocation is explicit using `std.heap.page_allocator.alloc`. The developer is directly responsible for allocating and freeing the memory, allowing for more control over memory usage and potentially better performance in critical sections compared to automatic garbage collection.[16]

4. The Necessity of Seamless Interoperability:

Problem: Modern software projects rarely start from scratch. They often need to integrate with existing libraries and systems, many of which are written in C. The complexity of Foreign Function Interfaces (FFIs) in some languages can make this integration challenging and error-prone.

Zig's Approach: Zig is designed for **excellent C interoperability**.[17] It can directly import C header files and call C functions with minimal overhead.[18] Zig's type system is designed to closely mirror C's, making the interface relatively straightforward. This allows developers to leverage the vast ecosystem of existing C libraries within their Zig projects without significant friction.

Example:

Code snippet

```
// Import the standard C library
```

```
extern "c" {
    fn puts(str: [*c]const u8) c_int;
}

pub fn main() !void {
    const message = "Hello from Zig calling C!";
    const result = puts(message.ptr);
    if (result == 0) {
        std.debug.print("C function 'puts' executed successfully.\n",
.{});
    } else {
        std.debug.print("Error calling C function 'puts'.\n", .{});
    }
}

const c_int = c"int"; // Define c_int for clarity
```

This simple example demonstrates how Zig can directly call the puts function from the standard C library. The extern "c" block allows Zig to interact with C code.

5. The Desire for Improved Tooling and Build Systems:

Problem: Setting up and managing build systems and dependencies can be a complex and time-consuming task in many languages. Inconsistent build systems and fragmented package management ecosystems can hinder productivity.

Zig's Approach: Zig includes a **built-in build system** and **package manager (zon).**[19] The build system is written in Zig itself, providing a consistent and powerful way to manage project dependencies, compilation, linking, and other build steps.[20]

Cross-compilation is also a first-class feature, making it easier to build software for different target platforms.[21]

Example (Conceptual - Build files are Zig code): A simplified conceptual view of a `build.zig` file might look like this:

Code snippet

```
const std = @import("std");

pub fn build(b: *std.build.Builder) !void {
    const target = b.standardTargetOptions(.{});
    const optimize = b.standardOptimizeOption(.{});

    const exe = b.addExecutable(.{
        .name = "my_app",
        .root_source_file = .{ .path = "src/main.zig" },
        .target = target,
        .optimize = optimize,
    });

    b.installArtifact(exe);
}
```

This shows how the build process is defined using Zig code, offering more flexibility and power compared to some traditional build systems.

In conclusion, Zig's design choices are a direct response to the challenges faced in modern software development. By prioritizing simplicity, explicitness, safety (without sacrificing performance), seamless C interoperability, and providing integrated tooling, Zig positions itself as a compelling language for professionals tackling complex and performance-critical projects.

1.2 Core Principles of the Zig Language: Simplicity, Safety, and Performance

Let's dive into the core principles that underpin the design of the Zig language: Simplicity, Safety, and Performance. These three pillars are not independent but rather deeply intertwined, influencing nearly every aspect of the language.

1. Simplicity:

The Goal: To reduce cognitive load on the developer, making the language easier to learn, understand, and maintain. Simplicity in Zig manifests in its minimal syntax, a small set of core concepts, and the absence of hidden control flow or implicit behavior. The idea is that what you see in the code is what you get at runtime.

Manifestations in Zig:

Minimal Syntax: Zig deliberately has a concise and consistent syntax. There are fewer keywords and language constructs compared to many other modern languages. This reduces the initial learning curve and makes code more uniform.

No Hidden Control Flow: Features like exceptions, which can cause non-local jumps in execution, are absent in Zig. Error handling is explicit through error unions. This makes the flow of execution easier to follow and reason about.

Explicit Memory Management: While manual, Zig's memory management is explicit. Allocation and deallocation are done through allocator interfaces, making it clear where and when memory operations are happening. There's no garbage collector running behind the scenes with unpredictable pauses.

Comptime for Metaprogramming: Zig's compile-time execution (`comptime`) allows for powerful metaprogramming without introducing a separate macro language. This keeps the metaprogramming constructs within the core language, enhancing simplicity.

Unified Calling Convention: Zig aims for a consistent calling convention, making it easier to understand how functions interact, especially when dealing with C interoperability.

Code Illustration:

Code snippet

```
// Simple function to add two integers
fn add(a: i32, b: i32) i32 {
    return a + b;
}

// Explicit error handling when opening a file
const std = @import("std");
const fs = std.fs;

pub fn readFile(path: []const u8) ![]u8 {
    const file = try fs.openFile(path, .{}) catch |err| return err;
    defer file.close();
```

```
                        const      contents      =        try
file.readToEndAlloc(std.heap.page_allocator);
    return contents;
}

pub fn main() !void {
    const sum = add(5, 3);
    std.debug.print("Sum: {}\n", .{sum});

    const fileResult = readFile("my_file.txt");
    if (fileResult) |contents| {
        std.debug.print("File contents: {}\n", .{contents});
        std.heap.page_allocator.free(contents);
    } else |err| {
        std.debug.print("Error: {}\n", .{err});
    }
}
```

In this example, the add function is straightforward. The readFile function demonstrates explicit error handling with the ! return type and the try...catch block. The memory allocation using std.heap.page_allocator.alloc (within readToEndAlloc) is also explicit.

2. Safety:

The Goal: To help developers write reliable and secure software by preventing common pitfalls like memory errors, data races, and undefined behavior. Zig achieves safety without imposing the overhead of a garbage collector, making it suitable for performance-critical applications.

Manifestations in Zig:

No Implicit Type Conversions: Zig requires explicit type casts, preventing unexpected data loss or misinterpretations that can arise from implicit conversions in other languages.

Optional Types (?T): These force developers to handle the possibility of a value being absent, reducing null pointer exceptions.

Error Unions (!T): As seen before, these make error handling a first-class citizen, ensuring that potential failures are considered and dealt with explicitly.

Bounds Checking (in Debug Builds): Zig performs bounds checking on array and slice accesses in debug builds, catching out-of-bounds errors early in development. This can be disabled for performance in release builds when the code is well-tested.

No Undefined Behavior (by default): Zig aims to eliminate many sources of undefined behavior common in C and C++, leading to more predictable and portable code.

Built-in Testing with Memory Safety Checks: The testing framework encourages writing tests that can also detect memory leaks and other memory-related issues.

Safer Concurrency Primitives: While Zig's concurrency model is still evolving, the design emphasizes safer ways to handle shared mutable state, often through message passing or explicit synchronization mechanisms.

Code Illustration:

Code snippet

```
// Explicit type casting
fn process(value: u32) void {
    const value_i64: i64 = @intCast(value); // Explicit cast required
    std.debug.print("Processed value: {}\n", .{value_i64});
}

// Optional type example
fn maybeGetName(id: u32) ?[]const u8 {
    if (id == 1) return "Charlie";
    return null;
}

pub fn main() !void {
    process(10);

    const name = maybeGetName(1);
    if (name) |n| {
        std.debug.print("Name: {}\n", .{n});
    } else {
        std.debug.print("Name not found.\n", .{});
    }

    // Potential out-of-bounds access (will panic in debug build)
    const array: [3]i32 = .{1, 2, 3};
    // std.debug.print("Element at index 5: {}\n", .{array[5]}); //
Uncommenting this would cause a panic in debug
```

```
}
```

The `process` function shows the need for an explicit cast using `@intCast`. The `maybeGetName` function uses an optional type `?[]const u8`, and the `main` function handles the potential `null` value. The commented-out line demonstrates a potential out-of-bounds access that Zig's debug mode would catch.

3. Performance:

The Goal: To enable developers to write highly efficient code that can run close to the metal, without the overhead of garbage collection or large runtime environments. Zig achieves this by giving developers fine-grained control over system resources while still providing safety nets.

Manifestations in Zig:

Manual Memory Management: Allows for precise control over memory allocation and deallocation, crucial for performance-critical applications where predictable memory usage is essential. Developers can choose different allocators tailored to specific needs.

No Hidden Control Flow: The explicitness of Zig's control flow makes it easier to reason about the performance implications of different code paths.

Low-Level Access: Zig provides mechanisms for direct interaction with hardware and low-level system APIs when needed.

SIMD Intrinsics: Zig exposes compiler intrinsics that allow developers to leverage Single Instruction, Multiple Data (SIMD) capabilities of modern processors for data-parallel computations.

Comptime for Optimization: Compile-time execution allows for optimizations like constant folding and code specialization to be performed before runtime, leading to more efficient executables.

Small Standard Library (Core Language Focus): The standard library provides essential functionalities without being overly bloated, keeping the runtime footprint small.

Cross-Compilation: Zig's excellent cross-compilation capabilities allow for building optimized binaries for specific target architectures.

Code Illustration (Illustrative - Performance optimization often involves more complex scenarios):

Code snippet

```
const std = @import("std");
const mem = std.mem;

// Manually allocate and copy memory
```

```
pub fn copyArrayManual(src: []const i32, dest: []i32) void {
    if (src.len != dest.len) {
        return;
    }
    for (0..src.len) |i| {
        dest[i] = src[i];
    }
}

pub fn main() !void {
    const source = [_]i32{1, 2, 3, 4, 5};
    var destination = [_]i32{0, 0, 0, 0, 0};

    copyArrayManual(&source, &destination);
        std.debug.print("Destination array (manual copy): {any}\n",
.{destination});

    // Using the standard library's optimized copy
    var destination2 = [_]i32{0, 0, 0, 0, 0};
    mem.copy(i32, &destination2, &source);
        std.debug.print("Destination array (mem.copy): {any}\n",
.{destination2});
}
```

This example shows both a manual memory copy and the use of the standard library's `mem.copy`, which is often highly optimized. In performance-critical scenarios, understanding memory layout and using appropriate allocation strategies can significantly impact speed. Zig gives you the control to make these choices.

In summary, Simplicity, Safety, and Performance are the guiding principles behind Zig's design. The language strives to achieve a balance between these three, offering a modern systems programming experience that is both powerful and approachable for professionals. The explicitness of the language contributes to both its simplicity and safety, while manual memory management and low-level access enable high performance.

1.3 Setting Up Your Professional Zig Development Environment

Let's break down setting up your Zig development environment in a simpler way, focusing on the essentials to get you started:

Think of it like setting up a workshop for building with Zig.

1.**Get the Zig Tools (Install Zig):**

Imagine you need a specific set of tools for woodworking. For Zig, the main tool is the `zig` command itself.

Go to the Zig website (https://ziglang.org/download/) and download the package for your computer (Windows, Mac, or Linux).

Installation is like unpacking your tools and putting them where you can easily reach them.

Windows: Unzip the downloaded folder to a place like `C:\Zig`. Then, tell your computer where to find these tools so you can use the `zig` command from anywhere. This is like adding the tools' location to your mental "where to find things" list. You do this by editing something called the "PATH" environment variable.

Mac/Linux: Unpack the downloaded file to a folder (like `/opt/zig` or a folder in your home directory). Then, you also need to tell your computer where to find the `zig` command by adding its location to your shell's configuration file (like `.zshrc` or `.bashrc`).

2. Check if the Tools Work (Verify Installation):

Once you've "unpacked" and told your computer where the Zig tools are, you need to make sure they work.

Open a new command prompt or terminal (the black screen where you type commands).

Type `zig version` and press Enter.

If you see a version number (like `0.13.0-dev.something`), it means your Zig tools are installed correctly and ready to use!

3. Organize Your Projects (Project Structure):

When you build things, it's good to keep your parts organized. For a Zig project, a common way to organize things is:

`my_project/`: This is the main folder for your project.

`build.zig`: This file is like the instructions for how to build your project (compile the code, etc.).

`src/`: This folder holds your main Zig code files (usually ending in `.zig`). The main program usually starts in a file called `main.zig`.

4. **Your First Simple Project ("Hello, World!"):**

Let's build a very basic program that just says "Hello, world!".

Create the folders and file:

Bash

```
mkdir hello_zig
cd hello_zig
mkdir src
```

Inside `src`, create a file named `main.zig` and put this code in it:

Code snippet

```
const std = @import("std");

pub fn main() !void {
    std.debug.print("Hello, world from Zig!\n", .{});
}
```

In the main `hello_zig` folder, create a file named `build.zig` and put this code in it:

Code snippet

```
const std = @import("std");

pub fn build(b: *std.build.Builder) !void {
    const target = b.standardTargetOptions(.{});
    const optimize = b.standardOptimizeOption(.{});

    const exe = b.addExecutable(.{
        .name = "hello_zig",
        .root_source_file = .{ .path = "src/main.zig" },
```

```
        .target = target,
        .optimize = optimize,
    });

    b.installArtifact(exe);
}
```

Now, to build and run this program, open your terminal in the `hello_zig` folder and type:

Bash

zig build run

You should see "Hello, world from Zig!" printed on your screen.

5. **Making Coding Easier (Editors and IDEs):**

Typing code in a plain text editor can be a bit basic. Special tools called editors or Integrated Development Environments (IDEs) can help you write code faster and with fewer mistakes.

VS Code: A popular free editor. You can add a "Zig Language Support" extension to it to get helpful features like highlighting your Zig code, suggesting code as you type, and checking for errors.

Other Options: There are other editors like IntelliJ IDEA (which might have a Zig plugin) and simpler text editors like Vim or Neovim (which can be configured for Zig).

6. Getting Extra Tools (Language Server - ZLS):

Think of a language server as a helpful assistant for your editor. It understands Zig code really well and can provide advanced features like:

Code Completion: Suggesting what to type next.

Error Checking: Pointing out mistakes as you write.

Jumping to Definitions: Quickly finding where a piece of code is defined.

The "Zig Language Support" extension for VS Code usually takes care of installing and setting up ZLS for you automatically.

7. Managing External Parts (Dependencies with zon):

Sometimes, your project will need to use code written by other people (like libraries for graphics or networking). These are called dependencies.

Zig has a tool called `zon` to help manage these.

To start using it in your project, you run `zig init-pkg` in your project folder. This creates a `build.zig.zon` file.

You list the dependencies you need in this file (like a shopping list).

Then, you run `zig build --fetch` to download these dependencies.

Finally, you tell your `build.zig` file to use these downloaded parts when building your project.

In simple terms:

Install Zig: Get your main Zig tool.

Project Structure: Keep your project organized.

"Hello, World!": Your first basic test.

Editor/IDE: A more helpful place to write code.

Language Server (ZLS): A smart assistant for your editor.

zon: Helps you get and manage extra code parts your project needs.

This should give you a more straightforward understanding of the steps involved in setting up your Zig development environment. As you get more comfortable, you can explore the more advanced options and configurations. Good luck with your Zig journey!

CHAPTER 2

Mastering the Fundamentals: Data Types, Variables, and Control Flow

2.1 Primitive Data Types and Their Nuances in Zig

Let's explore the primitive data types in Zig and their nuances. Primitive data types are the fundamental building blocks for representing values in the language. Zig offers a rich set of these, emphasizing explicitness and control over representation.

1. Integer Types:

Zig provides both signed and unsigned integer types with explicit bit widths.

Signed Integers: These can represent both positive and negative numbers. They are denoted by `i` followed by the number of bits (e.g., `i8`, `i16`, `i32`, `i64`, `i128`).

Unsigned Integers: These can only represent non-negative numbers (zero and positive). They are denoted by `u` followed by the number of bits (e.g., `u8`, `u16`, `u32`, `u64`, `u128`).

Architecture-Dependent Integers: Zig also offers `isize` and `usize`. Their size (in bits) depends on the target architecture (e.g., 32-bit on a 32-bit system, 64-bit on a 64-bit system). These are commonly used for indexing arrays and representing sizes.

Nuances of Integer Types:

Explicit Bit Width: Zig's insistence on explicit bit widths (e.g., `i32` vs. just `int`) promotes portability and makes the memory layout and potential range of values very clear. This contrasts with languages where the size of `int` can vary by platform.

Overflow Behavior: Zig provides different ways to handle integer overflow:

Wrapping: The default behavior in release builds is wrapping arithmetic. For example, `u8.add(255, 1)` will result in `0`.

Checked Arithmetic: You can use functions like `std.math.addExact`, `std.math.subExact`, etc., which return an error if overflow occurs.

Saturating Arithmetic: Functions like `std.math.addSat` will saturate at the maximum or minimum value instead of wrapping.

Unchecked Arithmetic: Using `@addUnchecked` (and similar intrinsics) bypasses overflow checks for maximum performance when you are certain overflow won't happen or have handled it manually.

Code snippet

```
const std = @import("std");
const math = std.math;

pub fn main() !void {
```

```
var a: u8 = 255;
a += 1; // Wraps to 0 in release mode

var b: u8 = 250;
const result_add = math.addExact(b, 10) catch |err| {
    std.debug.print("Overflow during addition: {}\n", .{err});
    return;
};
std.debug.print("Checked addition: {}\n", .{result_add});

var c: u8 = 250;
const result_sat = math.addSat(c, 10);
    std.debug.print("Saturating addition: {}\n", .{result_sat}); //
Output: 255

var d: u8 = 250;
const result_unchecked = @addUnchecked(d, 10);
std.debug.print("Unchecked addition: {}\n", .{result_unchecked});
// Output: 260 (may wrap depending on context)
}
```

Sign Conversion: Conversions between signed and unsigned integers require explicit casts using @intCast. This highlights the potential for data loss or misinterpretation when changing the signedness of a value.

Code snippet

```
const std = @import("std");
```

```
pub fn main() !void {
    const signed_val: i32 = -5;
    const unsigned_val: u32 = @intCast(signed_val);
    std.debug.print("Signed: {}, Unsigned (cast): {}\n", .{signed_val,
unsigned_val});   //  Output:  Signed:  -5,  Unsigned  (cast):
4294967291

    const unsigned_positive: u32 = 10;
    const signed_positive: i32 = @intCast(unsigned_positive);
            std.debug.print("Unsigned:  {},  Signed  (cast):  {}\n",
.{unsigned_positive,  signed_positive});  //  Output:  Unsigned:  10,
Signed (cast): 10
}
```

2. Floating-Point Types:

Zig provides standard IEEE 754 floating-point types:

f16 (half-precision)

f32 (single-precision)

f64 (double-precision)

f80 (extended precision - often mapped to f64 on many architectures)

f128 (quadruple-precision)

Nuances of Floating-Point Types:

Precision and Range: The different floating-point types offer varying levels of precision and representable ranges. Choosing the appropriate type is crucial for accuracy and performance.

Special Values: Zig supports IEEE 754 special values like NaN (Not a Number), positive infinity (`std.math.inf(f32)`), and negative infinity (`std.math.negInf(f32)`). Comparisons involving NaN always return `false` (except for `!=`).

Code snippet

```
const std = @import("std");
const math = std.math;

pub fn main() !void {
    const a: f32 = 1.0 / 0.0;
    const b: f32 = -1.0 / 0.0;
    const c: f32 = math.sqrt(-1.0);

    std.debug.print("Infinity: {}\n", .{a}); // Output: inf
    std.debug.print("Negative Infinity: {}\n", .{b}); // Output: -inf
    std.debug.print("NaN: {}\n", .{c}); // Output: nan
    std.debug.print("NaN == NaN: {}\n", .{c == c}); // Output: false
    std.debug.print("NaN != NaN: {}\n", .{c != c}); // Output: true
}
```

Approximate Comparisons: Due to the nature of floating-point representation, direct equality comparisons can be unreliable. It's often necessary to compare floating-point numbers with a small tolerance (epsilon). Zig's standard library provides utilities for this.

Code snippet

```
const std = @import("std");
const math = std.math;

pub fn main() !void {
    const x: f32 = 0.1 + 0.2;
    const y: f32 = 0.3;

    std.debug.print("x: {}, y: {}\n", .{x, y});
    std.debug.print("x == y: {}\n", .{x == y}); // Output: false (due to
floating-point inaccuracies)

    const epsilon: f32 = 0.00001;
    const diff = math.abs(x - y);
    std.debug.print("Absolute difference: {}\n", .{diff});
    std.debug.print("Within tolerance: {}\n", .{diff < epsilon}); //
Output: true
}
```

3. Boolean Type:

bool: Represents truth values, either true or false.

Nuances of Boolean Type:

No Implicit Conversion from Integers: Unlike some languages, Zig does not implicitly convert integers to booleans (e.g., 0 is not automatically `false`, and non-zero is not automatically `true`). You must use explicit comparisons.

Code snippet

```
const std = @import("std");

pub fn main() !void {
    const zero: i32 = 0;
    // const is_false: bool = zero; // This would be a compile error

    const is_false: bool = zero == 0;
    std.debug.print("Is zero false? {}\n", .{is_false}); // Output: true

    const one: i32 = 1;
    const is_true: bool = one != 0;
    std.debug.print("Is one true? {}\n", .{is_true}); // Output: true
}
```

Size: The size of `bool` in memory is not strictly defined as one bit. It's often aligned to a byte for efficiency. If you need a single bit flag, consider using bit fields within a struct or bitwise operations on an integer type.

4. The `void` Type:

void: Represents the absence of a value. It's commonly used as the return type of functions that don't return anything or as a placeholder in generic contexts.

Nuances of void **Type:**

Cannot Hold a Value: You cannot create a variable of type void. It signifies the lack of a value.

Pointer to Void (*void**):** A pointer to void is a special type that can point to any data type. However, to access the underlying data, you must cast it to a specific pointer type. This is often used for low-level memory manipulation or when dealing with generic data.

Code snippet

```
const std = @import("std");

fn printBytes(ptr: *const void, len: usize) void {
    const bytes = @ptrCast([*]const u8, ptr);
    for (0..len) |i| {
        std.debug.print("{x} ", .{bytes[i]});
    }
    std.debug.print("\n", .{});
}

pub fn main() !void {
    const numbers = [_]i32{1, 2, 3, 4, 5};
    printBytes(@ptrCast([*]const void, &numbers), numbers.len * @sizeOf(i32));

    const message = "Hello";
```

```
    printBytes(@ptrCast([*]const void, message.ptr), message.len);
}
```

5. The anyopaque Type:

anyopaque: Represents a type whose size and layout are unknown at compile time. It's primarily used for interacting with external (e.g., C) code where the exact structure might not be fully known or when dealing with highly abstract interfaces.

Nuances of anyopaque Type:

Limited Operations: You can't directly access fields or perform many operations on anyopaque types. You typically need to cast them to a concrete pointer type to interact with the underlying data.

Common in FFI: Often used when defining bindings to C structures or opaque pointers.

6. The type Type:

type: Represents a type itself as a first-class value. This enables powerful metaprogramming capabilities in Zig.

Nuances of type Type:

Compile-Time Introspection: You can inspect and manipulate types at compile time using @TypeOf and other reflection-like features.

Generic Programming: `type` is fundamental for writing generic functions and data structures that can work with different types.

Code snippet

```
const std = @import("std");

fn printTypeName(comptime T: type) void {
    std.debug.print("The type is: {}\n", .{@typeName(T)});
}

pub fn main() !void {
    printTypeName(i32); // Output: The type is: i32
    printTypeName(f64); // Output: The type is: f64
    printTypeName([3]u8); // Output: The type is: [3]u8
}
```

Understanding these primitive data types and their nuances is crucial for writing correct, efficient, and portable Zig code. Zig's emphasis on explicitness empowers developers with fine-grained control over data representation and behavior.

2.2 Variables, Mutability, and Memory Management Fundamentals

Alright, let's delve into the fundamentals of variables, mutability, and memory management in Zig. These concepts are foundational to any programming language, and Zig has some distinct characteristics in how it handles them, emphasizing explicitness and control.

1. Variables:

Declaration: In Zig, you declare variables using the `var` keyword, followed by the variable name, an optional explicit type, and an optional initializer. If you don't provide a type, Zig can often infer it from the initializer.

Code snippet

```
var count: i32 = 0; // Explicit type and initializer
var message = "Hello"; // Type inferred as []const u8
var is_active: bool; // Explicit type, no initializer (will have a default
value of false)
```

Type Inference: Zig's type inference can be convenient, but it's generally good practice in professional code to be explicit with types, especially for clarity and to avoid unexpected type mismatches.

Scope: Variables in Zig have block scope. They are only accessible within the block of code (defined by curly braces {}) where they are declared.

Code snippet

```
const std = @import("std");
```

```zig
pub fn main() !void {
    var x: i32 = 10;
    {
        var y: i32 = 20;
        std.debug.print("Inside block: x = {}, y = {}\n", .{x, y}); // x and
y are accessible
    }
    std.debug.print("Outside block: x = {}\n", .{x}); // x is accessible,
y is not
    // std.debug.print("Outside block: y = {}\n", .{y}); // This would be
a compile error
}
```

2. Mutability:

Immutability by Default: In Zig, variables declared with `const` are immutable, meaning their value cannot be changed after initialization. This promotes safer and more predictable code.

Code snippet

```zig
const pi: f64 = 3.14159;
// pi = 3.0; // This would be a compile error
```

Explicit Mutability: To declare a mutable variable (one whose value can be changed), you must use the `var` keyword.

Code snippet

```
var counter: i32 = 0;
counter = counter + 1; // This is allowed
std.debug.print("Counter: {}\n", .{counter}); // Output: Counter: 1
```

Mutability and Pointers: The mutability of a variable and the mutability of a pointer to that variable are distinct concepts. A `const` pointer can point to a `var` variable, and a `var` pointer can point to a `const` variable (with appropriate casting). However, you can only modify the value through a `var` pointer.

Code snippet

```
const std = @import("std");

pub fn main() !void {
    var value: i32 = 5;
    const const_ptr: *const i32 = &value; // Constant pointer to a mutable variable
    var var_ptr: *i32 = &value;          // Mutable pointer to a mutable variable
    const const_val: i32 = 10;
    var var_ptr_to_const: *const i32 = &const_val; // Mutable pointer to a constant variable (requires cast to modify)
```

```
    std.debug.print("Initial value: {}\n", .{value}); // Output: Initial
value: 5

    var_ptr.* = 15; // Modifying through the mutable pointer
    std.debug.print("Value after var_ptr modification: {}\n", .{value});
// Output: Value after var_ptr modification: 15

    // const_ptr.* = 20; // This would be a compile error (cannot
modify through a const pointer)

    // var_ptr_to_const.* = 25; // This would also be a compile error
(cannot modify a const value through any pointer without a cast,
and even then, it's generally unsafe)
}
```

3. Memory Management Fundamentals:

Zig provides **manual memory management**. This means you, the developer, are responsible for explicitly allocating and deallocating memory. While this gives you fine-grained control for performance, it also requires careful attention to avoid memory leaks, dangling pointers, and other memory-related errors.

Allocators: Zig uses the concept of **allocators** to manage memory. An allocator is an object that provides functions for allocating and deallocating blocks of memory. The standard library (`std.mem`) provides several built-in allocators.

Common Allocators:

`std.heap.GeneralPurposeAllocator(.{})`: A general-purpose heap allocator. You need to initialize it with a memory arena.

`std.heap.ArenaAllocator`: An allocator that allocates from a specific memory arena. All allocations from an arena are freed at once when the arena is deinitialized. Useful for managing memory within a specific scope or operation.

`std.heap.FixedBufferAllocator`: Allocates from a fixed-size buffer provided at initialization. Useful for stack-like allocation within a limited space.

`std.heap.PageAllocator`: A simple page-based allocator.

`std.testing.allocator`: A special allocator used for testing to track allocations and detect leaks.

Allocation and Deallocation:

To allocate memory, you typically use the `alloc` method of an allocator, specifying the number of elements and the type of each element. This returns a pointer to the allocated memory.

To deallocate memory, you use the `free` method of the *same* allocator that was used for allocation, passing the pointer to the allocated memory.

It's crucial to pair every allocation with a corresponding deallocation to prevent memory leaks. The `defer` keyword in Zig is very useful for ensuring deallocation happens, even if errors occur.

Code snippet

```
const std = @import("std");

pub fn main() !void {
    var gpa = std.heap.GeneralPurposeAllocator(.{}){};
    defer gpa.deinit();
    const allocator = gpa.allocator();

    // Allocate an array of 5 i32 values
    const array = try allocator.alloc(i32, 5);
    defer allocator.free(array); // Ensure memory is freed when the
function exits

    // Initialize the array
    for (0..array.len) |i| {
        array[i] = @intCast(i32, i * 2);
    }
    std.debug.print("Allocated array: {any}\n", .{array});

    // Allocate a string
    const message = try allocator.alloc(u8, 12);
    defer allocator.free(message);
    std.mem.copy(u8, message, "Hello Zig!");
    std.debug.print("Allocated string: {s}\n", .{message});
}
```

Slices: Zig uses slices ([ ]T) to represent dynamically sized views into contiguous blocks of memory (which could be stack-allocated arrays or heap-allocated memory). Slices themselves do not own the memory; they are just a pointer and a length. This allows for flexible ways to work with data without always needing to allocate.

Code snippet

```
const std = @import("std");

pub fn main() !void {
    const static_array = [_]i32{10, 20, 30, 40};
    const slice: []const i32 = static_array[1..3]; // A slice of the static array

    std.debug.print("Slice: {any}\n", .{slice}); // Output: Slice: [20, 30]

    var gpa = std.heap.GeneralPurposeAllocator(.{}){};
    defer gpa.deinit();
    const allocator = gpa.allocator();

    const dynamic_array = try allocator.alloc(i32, 3);
    defer allocator.free(dynamic_array);
    dynamic_array[0] = 100;
    dynamic_array[1] = 200;
    dynamic_array[2] = 300;

    const dynamic_slice: []i32 = dynamic_array; // A slice of the heap-allocated array
    std.debug.print("Dynamic Slice: {any}\n", .{dynamic_slice}); // Output: Dynamic Slice: [100, 200, 300]
```

}

Stack Allocation: Zig also allows for stack-based allocation, which is generally faster than heap allocation. Variables declared within a function without explicit allocation using an allocator are typically stack-allocated. The memory for these variables is automatically managed when the function exits.

Code snippet

```
const std = @import("std");

fn processData() void {
    var buffer: [1024]u8 = undefined; // Stack-allocated buffer
    const message: []const u8 = "Data to store";
    std.mem.copy(u8, &buffer, message);
    std.debug.print("Data on stack: {s}\n", .{&buffer});
}

pub fn main() !void {
    processData();
}
```

Key Takeaways for Memory Management in Zig:

Manual is Explicit: You are in control of when memory is allocated and deallocated.

Use Allocators: Memory is managed through allocator objects.

Pair Allocate and Free: Every call to `alloc` (or similar allocation functions) must have a corresponding `free`.

`defer` **for Safety:** Use `defer` to ensure deallocation happens automatically when the scope is exited.

Slices are Views: Slices provide flexible access to memory without ownership.

Stack for Simplicity: Use stack allocation for automatic memory management within function scopes when the size is known at compile time.

Understanding these fundamentals of variables, mutability, and Zig's manual memory management model is crucial for writing robust and efficient Zig applications. The explicitness of the language in these areas empowers developers but also requires careful attention to detail.

2.3 Control Flow Structures: if, else, while, for, and Error Handling

Alright, let's explore the control flow structures in Zig: `if`, `else`, `while`, `for`, and how error handling integrates with these constructs. These are essential for creating logic and making decisions within your Zig programs.

1. `if` **and** `else` **Statements:**

The `if` statement in Zig allows you to execute a block of code conditionally based on a boolean expression. An optional `else` block can be provided to execute code if the condition is false. You can also chain conditions using `else if`.

Basic `if`:

Code snippet

```
const std = @import("std");

pub fn main() !void {
    const age = 25;
    if (age >= 18) {
        std.debug.print("You are an adult.\n", .{});
    }
}
```

`if` **with** `else`**:**

Code snippet

```
const std = @import("std");

pub fn main() !void {
    const temperature = 15.0;
    if (temperature > 20.0) {
        std.debug.print("It's warm.\n", .{});
```

```
} else {
    std.debug.print("It's cool.\n", .{});
}
}
```

if, else if, else:

Code snippet

```
const std = @import("std");

pub fn main() !void {
    const grade = 85;
    if (grade >= 90) {
        std.debug.print("Grade: A\n", .{});
    } else if (grade >= 80) {
        std.debug.print("Grade: B\n", .{});
    } else if (grade >= 70) {
        std.debug.print("Grade: C\n", .{});
    } else {
        std.debug.print("Grade: Below C\n", .{});
    }
}
```

if **as an Expression:** In Zig, if can also be used as an expression that evaluates to a value. The else branch is mandatory in this case, and both branches must have compatible types.

Code snippet

```
const std = @import("std");

pub fn main() !void {
    const is_even = true;
    const message = if (is_even) "The number is even." else "The number is odd.";
    std.debug.print("{s}\n", .{message}); // Output: The number is even.

    const age = 15;
    const status = if (age >= 18) "Adult" else "Minor";
    std.debug.print("Status: {s}\n", .{status}); // Output: Status: Minor
}
```

2. while **Loops:**

The while loop in Zig executes a block of code repeatedly as long as a specified boolean condition is true.

Basic while**:**

Code snippet

```
const std = @import("std");

pub fn main() !void {
    var counter: i32 = 0;
    while (counter < 5) {
        std.debug.print("Counter is: {}\n", .{counter});
        counter += 1;
    }
    std.debug.print("Loop finished.\n", .{});
}
```

break **and** continue: You can use break to exit a while loop prematurely and continue to skip the rest of the current iteration and proceed to the next condition check.

Code snippet

```
const std = @import("std");

pub fn main() !void {
    var i: i32 = 0;
    while (i < 10) {
        i += 1;
        if (i % 2 == 0) {
            continue; // Skip even numbers
        }
        std.debug.print("Odd number: {}\n", .{i});
        if (i == 7) {
            break; // Exit the loop when i is 7
```

```
}
    }
    std.debug.print("Loop ended.\n", .{});
}
```

3. `for` Loops:

Zig provides a flexible `for` loop that can iterate over ranges, arrays, slices, and more.

Iterating over a Range:

Code snippet

```
const std = @import("std");

pub fn main() !void {
    for (0..5) |i| {
        std.debug.print("Index: {}\n", .{i}); // Iterates from 0 up to (but
not including) 5
    }
}
```

Iterating over an Array or Slice:

Code snippet

```
const std = @import("std");

pub fn main() !void {
    const numbers = [_]i32{10, 20, 30, 40};
    for (numbers) |number| {
        std.debug.print("Number: {}\n", .{number}); // Iterates over the
values
    }

    const colors = [_][]const u8{"red", "green", "blue"};
    for (colors, 0..) |color, index| {
        std.debug.print("Color at index {}: {}\n", .{index, color}); //
Iterates with index
    }
}
```

break **and** continue **in** for **loops:** These keywords work similarly to while loops.

4. Error Handling with try **and** catch:

Zig's error handling is explicit using error unions (!T). The try keyword is used to call a function that can return an error. If an error is returned, the execution jumps to the nearest catch block.

Basic try...catch:

Code snippet

```zig
const std = @import("std");
const fs = std.fs;

pub fn readFile(path: []const u8) ![]u8 {
    const file = try fs.openFile(path, .{}) catch |err| {
        std.debug.print("Error opening file: {}\n", .{err});
        return err; // Re-propagate the error
    };
    defer file.close();
    const contents = try file.readToEndAlloc(std.heap.page_allocator);
    return contents;
}

pub fn main() !void {
    const result = readFile("non_existent_file.txt") catch |err| {
        std.debug.print("Main function caught error: {}\n", .{err});
        return;
    };

    if (result) |contents| {
        std.debug.print("File contents: {}\n", .{contents});
        std.heap.page_allocator.free(contents);
    }
}
```

In this example, if `fs.openFile` or `file.readToEndAlloc` returns an error, the execution jumps to the `catch` block immediately following the `try`. The error value can be captured using `|err|` within the `catch` block.

catch **with Specific Errors:** You can catch specific errors by specifying them after the `catch` keyword.

Code snippet

```
const std = @import("std");
const fs = std.fs;
const builtin = @import("builtin");

pub fn readFile(path: []const u8) ![]u8 {
    const file = try fs.openFile(path, .{}) catch |err| switch (err) {
        error.FileNotFound => {
            std.debug.print("File not found: {}\n", .{path});
            return err;
        },
        else => {
            std.debug.print("Error opening file: {}\n", .{err});
            return err;
        },
    };
    defer file.close();
    const         contents      =      try
file.readToEndAlloc(std.heap.page_allocator);
    return contents;
}

pub fn main() !void {
    _ = readFile("missing.txt") catch unreachable;
}
```

try within if and other control flow: `try` can be used within `if` conditions or other control flow structures when dealing with functions that return error unions.

Code snippet

```
const std = @import("std");
const parseInt = std.fmt.parseInt;

pub fn main() !void {
    const input = "123";
    const result = parseInt(i32, input, 10) catch |err| {
        std.debug.print("Error parsing integer: {}\n", .{err});
        return;
    };

    if (result > 100) {
        std.debug.print("Parsed value is greater than 100: {}\n",
.{result});
    } else {
        std.debug.print("Parsed value is not greater than 100: {}\n",
.{result});
    }
}
```

Key Aspects of Control Flow in Zig:

Familiar Structures: `if`, `else`, `while`, and `for` behave in ways that are generally familiar to programmers from other languages.

if as Expression: The ability to use `if` as an expression can lead to more concise code in certain situations.

Explicit Error Handling: Error handling with `try` and `catch` is tightly integrated with the language through error unions, promoting robust code.

Iteration Flexibility: The `for` loop offers powerful ways to iterate over various data structures and ranges.

`break` **and** `continue`**:** These provide control over the execution flow within loops.

Mastering these control flow structures and Zig's explicit error handling mechanism is fundamental for writing programs that can make decisions, repeat actions, and gracefully handle potential failures.

CHAPTER 3

Functions, Structs, and Enums: Building Blocks of Zig Applications

3.1 Defining and Utilizing Functions: Parameters, Return Types, and Calling Conventions

Alright, let's explore how to define and utilize functions in Zig, covering parameters, return types, and the basics of calling conventions. Functions are the fundamental building blocks for organizing and reusing code.

1. Defining Functions:

In Zig, you define a function using the `fn` keyword, followed by the function name, a list of parameters enclosed in parentheses, an optional return type, and the function body enclosed in curly braces {}.

Code snippet

```
fn add(a: i32, b: i32) i32 {
    const sum: i32 = a + b;
    return sum;
}
```

`fn add`: Declares a function named `add`.

`(a: i32, b: i32)`: Defines the parameters. `a` and `b` are the parameter names, and `i32` is the type of each parameter. Parameters are separated by commas.

`i32`: Specifies the return type of the function. In this case, the function returns a 32-bit signed integer. If a function doesn't return a value, the return type is `void`.

`{ ... }`: Encloses the body of the function, containing the statements to be executed.

2. Parameters:

Functions can accept zero or more parameters. Each parameter has a name and a type.

Multiple Parameters: As seen in the `add` example, multiple parameters are separated by commas.

No Parameters: If a function doesn't take any arguments, the parentheses are empty:

Code snippet

```
fn greet() void {
    const std = @import("std");
    std.debug.print("Hello!\n", .{});
}
```

Variadic Parameters (Comptime VarArgs): Zig supports compile-time variadic arguments using the `...` syntax with a comptime type. This is often used for functions like `std.debug.print`.

Code snippet

```
fn printMany(comptime format: []const u8, args: ...) void {
    const std = @import("std");
    std.debug.print(format, args);
}

pub fn main() !void {
    printMany("Name: {}, Age: {}\n", .{"Alice", 30});
    printMany("Value: {}\n", .{123});
}
```

3. Return Types:

Functions can return a single value of a specified type.

Explicit Return: The `return` keyword is used to exit a function and optionally provide a return value. The type of the returned expression must match the function's declared return type.

No Return Value (`void`): If a function doesn't return a value, its return type is `void`. The `return` keyword can be used without an expression to exit the function.

Code snippet

```
fn printAndExit(code: i32) void {
    const std = @import("std");
    std.debug.print("Exiting with code: {}\n", .{code});
    return; // Optional return statement for void functions
}
```

Error Unions (!T): Functions that can fail often return an error union. The ! before a type indicates that the function can return either a value of that type or an error. You use try to handle the potential error.

Code snippet

```
const std = @import("std");
const fs = std.fs;

fn readFile(path: []const u8) ![]u8 {
    const file = try fs.openFile(path, .{}) catch |err| return err;
    defer file.close();
    const contents = try file.readToEndAlloc(std.heap.page_allocator);
    return contents;
}
```

Optional Types (?T): If a function might return a value or nothing (null-like), you can use an optional return type.

Code snippet

```
fn findUserById(id: u32) ?User {
    // Simulate finding a user; might return null if not found
    if (id == 123) {
        return User{ .id = 123, .name = "Alice" };
    } else {
        return null;
    }
}

const User = struct {
    id: u32,
    name: []const u8,
};
```

4. Calling Functions:

To execute a function, you "call" it by using its name followed by parentheses ( ). If the function has parameters, you provide the[1] arguments (values) inside the parentheses, matching the number and types of the parameters defined in the function signature.

Code snippet

```
const std = @import("std");

fn multiply(a: i32, b: i32) i32 {
    return a * b;
}

fn greetByName(name: []const u8) void {
    std.debug.print("Hello, {s}!\n", .{name});
}

pub fn main() !void {
    const product = multiply(5, 10); // Calling multiply with
arguments 5 and 10
    std.debug.print("Product: {}\n", .{product}); // Output: Product: 50

    greetByName("Bob"); // Calling greetByName with the argument
"Bob"
    // Output: Hello, Bob!

    const maybe_user = findUserById(123); // Calling findUserById
    if (maybe_user) |user| {
        std.debug.print("Found user: {}\n", .{user.name}); // Output:
Found user: Alice
    } else {
        std.debug.print("User not found.\n", .{});
    }

    const file_contents = readFile("my_file.txt") catch |err| {
        std.debug.print("Error reading file in main: {}\n", .{err});
        return;
    };
    if (file_contents) |contents| {
        std.debug.print("File content in main: {s}\n", .{contents});
        std.heap.page_allocator.free(contents);
    }
```

```
}
```

// (Assuming the User struct and readFile function are defined as in previous examples)

5. Calling Conventions (Basics):

Calling conventions define how arguments are passed to a function and how the return value is handled. While Zig aims for a consistent internal calling convention, when interacting with external code (like C libraries), understanding calling conventions becomes more important.

Zig's Internal Convention: Zig generally aims for an efficient and platform-dependent calling convention for its own functions. The specifics might vary based on the target architecture and optimization levels. For most pure-Zig code, you don't need to worry too much about the low-level details of how arguments are passed (registers vs. stack, etc.). The compiler handles this for you.

External Calling Conventions (extern): When interfacing with code written in other languages (primarily C using extern "c"), you are dealing with their calling conventions. The extern "c" keyword tells the Zig compiler to use the C calling convention for the declared external function. This ensures compatibility in how arguments are passed and the return value is handled.

Code snippet


```
extern "c" {
    fn c_function(arg1: i32, arg2: *const u8) i32;
}
```

```
pub fn main() !void {
    const result = c_function(10, "Hello".ptr);
    std.debug.print("Result from C function: {}\n", .{result});
}
```

In this example, `extern "c"` specifies that `c_function` follows the C calling convention.

Function Pointers and Calling Conventions: Function pointers in Zig can also have explicit calling conventions specified in their type. This is crucial when you have a function pointer that might point to a function with a different calling convention (though this is less common in typical Zig-to-Zig interactions).

Code snippet

```
const std = @import("std");

fn zigFunction(a: i32) i32 {
    return a * 2;
}

extern "c" fn cFunction(b: i32) i32; // Assume this is a C function

pub fn main() !void {
    const zig_fn_ptr: fn(i32) i32 = zigFunction;
    const c_fn_ptr: extern "c" fn(i32) i32 = cFunction;

    std.debug.print("Zig function call: {}\n", .{zig_fn_ptr(5)});
```

```
// std.debug.print("C function call: {}\n", .{c_fn_ptr(10)}); // Would
need actual C code linked
}
```

In summary, defining and utilizing functions in Zig involves specifying parameters with their types, an optional return type (which can include error unions or optionals), and a function body. Calling functions requires providing arguments that match the parameter types. While Zig handles its internal calling conventions for efficiency, you need to be aware of external calling conventions (like the C convention) when interoperating with code from other languages. Understanding these concepts is essential for structuring your Zig code into reusable and maintainable units.

3.2 Structs and Unions: Defining Custom Data Structures for Efficiency

Alright, let's dive into structs and unions in Zig, which are fundamental for defining your own custom data structures to represent complex entities and optimize memory usage.

1. Structs (Structures):

A struct in Zig is a composite data type that groups together zero or more variables (fields) under a single name.[1] The fields can be of different types. Structs are used to represent records or objects with a fixed set of attributes.

Defining a Struct: You define a struct using the struct keyword, followed by the struct name and a block {} containing the field definitions.[2] Each field definition specifies the field name and its type.

Code snippet

```
const std = @import("std");

struct Person {
    name: []const u8,
    age: u32,
    is_employed: bool,
}

pub fn main() !void {
    const alice = Person{
        .name = "Alice",
        .age = 30,
        .is_employed = true,
    };

        std.debug.print("Name: {s}, Age: {}, Employed: {}\n",
.{alice.name, alice.age, alice.is_employed});

    var bob = Person{
        .name = "Bob",
        .age = 25,
        .is_employed = false,
    };
    bob.is_employed = true; // Fields of a var struct can be modified
        std.debug.print("Name: {s}, Age: {}, Employed: {}\n",
.{bob.name, bob.age, bob.is_employed});
}
```

Anonymous Structs: You can also define structs without a name directly within a variable declaration or function parameter.

Code snippet

```
const std = @import("std");

pub fn main() !void {
    const point = struct { x: f32, y: f32 }{ .x = 1.0, .y = 2.5 };
    std.debug.print("Point: {{ x: {}, y: {} }}\n", .{point.x, point.y});
}
```

Packed Structs: By default, the Zig compiler might add padding between struct fields to ensure proper memory alignment for the target architecture, which can sometimes waste space. You can use the `packed` keyword before `struct` to instruct the compiler to remove this padding, potentially making the struct smaller in memory.[3] However, accessing fields in a packed struct might be slightly slower on some architectures.

Code snippet

```
const std = @import("std");

packed struct Data {
    a: u1, // 1-bit integer
    b: u2, // 2-bit integer
    c: u5, // 5-bit integer
```

```
}

pub fn main() !void {
    const data = Data{ .a = 1, .b = 2, .c = 30 };
    std.debug.print("Data: {{ a: {}, b: {}, c: {} }}\n", .{data.a, data.b,
data.c});
    std.debug.print("Size of Data: {} bytes\n", .{@sizeOf(Data)}); //
Size will likely be 1 byte
}
```

2. Unions:

A union in Zig is a data type that can hold one of several different types at the same memory location.[4] The size of the union is determined by the size of its largest field. Only one field of a union is active at any given time. Unions are useful for representing data that can take on different forms.

Defining a Union: You define a union using the `union` keyword, followed by the union name and a block `{}` containing the field definitions.

Code snippet

```
const std = @import("std");

union Value {
    int_val: i32,
    float_val: f32,
    text_val: []const u8,
```

```
}

pub fn main() !void {
    var v: Value = .{ .int_val = 10 };
    std.debug.print("Value (as int): {}\n", .{v.int_val});

    v.float_val = 3.14; // Now the float_val field is active
    std.debug.print("Value (as float): {}\n", .{v.float_val});

    v.text_val = "Hello"; // Now the text_val field is active
    std.debug.print("Value (as text): {s}\n", .{v.text_val});

    // std.debug.print("Value (as int again - might be garbage): {}\n",
.{v.int_val});
}
```

Tagged Unions (Enums with Data): A common and safer way to use unions is to combine them with an enum that indicates which field of the union is currently active. This is known as a tagged union or discriminated union. Zig provides a concise syntax for this.

Code snippet

```
const std = @import("std");

const Result = union(enum) {
    ok: []const u8,
    err: Error,
};

const Error = enum {
```

```
    FileNotFound,
    NetworkError,
    UnknownError,
};

pub fn main() !void {
    const success: Result = .{ .ok = "Data received" };
    const failure: Result = .{ .err = .NetworkError };

    printResult(success); // Output: OK: Data received
    printResult(failure); // Output: Error: NetworkError
}

fn printResult(result: Result) void {
    switch (result) {
        .ok => |data| {
            std.debug.print("OK: {s}\n", .{data});
        },
        .err => |error| {
            std.debug.print("Error: {}\n", .{error});
        },
    }
}
```

In this tagged union, the anonymous enum determines which field (ok or err) is active.[5] The switch statement safely accesses the active field.

Efficiency Considerations:

Memory Layout and Alignment (Structs): Understanding how the compiler lays out struct fields in memory and the potential padding is important for optimizing memory usage, especially in performance-critical applications or when interfacing with external data formats. Packed structs can help reduce size but might impact access speed. You can use `@sizeOf()` and `@alignOf()` to inspect the size and alignment of types.

Code snippet

```
const std = @import("std");

struct Example {
    a: u1,
    b: u32,
    c: u8,
}

packed struct PackedExample {
    a: u1,
    b: u32,
    c: u8,
}

pub fn main() !void {
    std.debug.print("Size of Example: {} bytes, Alignment: {} bytes\n", .{@sizeOf(Example), @alignOf(Example)});
    std.debug.print("Size of PackedExample: {} bytes, Alignment: {} bytes\n", .{@sizeOf(PackedExample), @alignOf(PackedExample)});
}
```

Memory Sharing (Unions): Unions are inherently memory-efficient when you have data that can exist in one of several forms but only one at a time. They allow you to reuse the same memory location for different types, reducing overall memory footprint. Tagged unions add a small overhead for the tag but provide type safety and prevent misinterpretation of the union's content.[6]

Choosing Between Struct and Union:

Use **structs** when you need to group together a fixed set of named fields that represent different attributes of an entity, and all these attributes are typically valid and accessed together.

Use **unions** when a variable can hold one of several different types of values, but only one at a time. Consider using tagged unions for safer and more maintainable code.

Arrays of Structs vs. Structs of Arrays: When dealing with collections of data, you might have a choice between an array of structs (e.g., `[100]Person`) or a struct of arrays (e.g., `struct { names: [100][]const u8, ages: [100]u32, ... }`). The optimal choice depends on how you intend to access and process the data. An array of structs is often better when you process each entity as a whole, while a struct of arrays can be more efficient for operations that iterate over a specific attribute across all entities (better cache locality).

Understanding how to define and utilize structs and unions effectively is crucial for designing efficient and well-organized data structures in Zig, allowing you to model your application's data appropriately and optimize for both memory usage and performance. The explicitness of packed structs and the safety of tagged unions provide powerful tools for fine-grained control over data representation.

3.3 Enums and Tagged Unions: Representing State and Choices Safely

Alright, let's delve into enums and tagged unions in Zig, which are powerful features for representing a finite set of states or choices in a type-safe and expressive manner. Tagged unions, in particular, enhance the safety and clarity of working with data that can take on different forms.

1. Enums (Enumerations):

An enum in Zig defines a type that has a fixed set of named values (members).[1] These members are typically used to represent distinct states, options, or categories within your program.

Basic Enum Definition: You define an enum using the enum keyword, followed by the enum name and a block {} containing the names of the members.

Code snippet

```
const std = @import("std");

const Color = enum {
    red,
    green,
    blue,
};

pub fn main() !void {
    const favorite_color: Color = .blue;
```

```
    if (favorite_color == .blue) {
        std.debug.print("My favorite color is blue.\n", .{});
    } else {
        std.debug.print("My favorite color is not blue.\n", .{});
    }

    switch (favorite_color) {
        .red => std.debug.print("It's red.\n", .{}),
        .green => std.debug.print("It's green.\n", .{}),
        .blue => std.debug.print("It's blue.\n", .{}),
    }
}
```

Explicit Values: You can explicitly assign integer values to enum members if needed. If you don't, Zig will automatically assign them starting from 0.

Code snippet

```
const Status = enum(i32) {
    ok = 200,
    not_found = 404,
    server_error = 500,
};

pub fn main() !void {
    const response_status: Status = .ok;
        std.debug.print("Status code: {}\n", .{response_status}); //
Output: Status code: 200
```

```
}
```

Underlying Type: You can specify the underlying integer type for an enum in the parentheses after the `enum` keyword (e.g., `enum(u8)`).[2] This can be useful for interoperability with C or when you need a specific size for the enum. If no type is specified, Zig chooses a suitable integer type based on the number of members.

2. Tagged Unions (Discriminated Unions):

A tagged union is a powerful pattern that combines an enum (the "tag") with a union. The enum indicates which of the union's fields is currently active. This provides a type-safe way to work with data that can have different structures or types depending on its state.

Basic Tagged Union Definition: In Zig, you define a tagged union using the `union(enum)` syntax. The enum is often anonymous and defined directly within the union definition. Each member of the enum corresponds to a field in the union.

Code snippet

```
const std = @import("std");

const OperationResult = union(enum) {
    success: i32,
    error: []const u8,
};

pub fn main() !void {
```

```
    const successful_result: OperationResult = .{ .success = 42 };
    const error_result: OperationResult = .{ .error = "Something
went wrong" };

    printOperationResult(successful_result); // Output: Success: 42
    printOperationResult(error_result);      // Output: Error:
Something went wrong
}

fn printOperationResult(result: OperationResult) void {
    switch (result) {
        .success => |value| {
            std.debug.print("Success: {}\n", .{value});
        },
        .error => |message| {
            std.debug.print("Error: {s}\n", .{message});
        },
    }
}
```

Here, `OperationResult` is a tagged union. The anonymous enum has two members: `success` and `error`. The union has corresponding fields: `success` (of type `i32`) and `error` (of type `[]const u8`). When you create a value of `OperationResult`, you specify which tag is active using the `.{ .tag = value }` syntax (or the shorthand `.tag = value` when the tag name matches the field name). The `switch` statement on the tagged union safely accesses the active field.

More Complex Tagged Unions: Tagged unions can have more than two variants, each with different data types.

Code snippet

```
const std = @import("std");

const Shape = union(enum) {
    circle: struct { radius: f32 },
    rectangle: struct { width: f32, height: f32 },
    triangle: struct { base: f32, height: f32 },
};

pub fn main() !void {
    const my_circle: Shape = .{ .circle = .{ .radius = 5.0 } };
    const my_rectangle: Shape = .{ .rectangle = .{ .width = 4.0,
.height = 6.0 } };

    printShapeArea(my_circle);      // Output: Area of circle:
78.539818
    printShapeArea(my_rectangle); // Output: Area of rectangle:
24.0
    // printShapeArea(.{ .triangle = .{ .base = 3.0, .height = 8.0 } });
}

fn printShapeArea(shape: Shape) void {
    switch (shape) {
        .circle => |c| {
            const area = std.math.pi * c.radius * c.radius;
            std.debug.print("Area of circle: {}\n", .{area});
        },
        .rectangle => |r| {
            const area = r.width * r.height;
            std.debug.print("Area of rectangle: {}\n", .{area});
        },
        .triangle => |t| {
            const area = 0.5 * t.base * t.height;
```

```
        std.debug.print("Area of triangle: {}\n", .{area});
    },
  }
}
```

Safety Benefits of Tagged Unions:

Type Safety: The compiler enforces that you handle all possible cases in a `switch` statement on a tagged union. This prevents you from accidentally treating a value as the wrong variant.

Clarity: The tag explicitly indicates the current state or type of the data within the union, making the code easier to understand and maintain.

Preventing Errors: Tagged unions help avoid common errors associated with regular unions, where you might access the wrong field and get garbage data or misinterpret the value.

Optional Tagged Unions: You can also have optional tagged unions using the `?` syntax.[3] This represents a tagged union that might also be `null`.

Code snippet

```
const std = @import("std");
```

```
const MaybeResult = ?union(enum) {
    value: i32,
    none: void,
};

pub fn main() !void {
    const has_value: MaybeResult = .{ .value = 100 };
    const no_value: MaybeResult = null;

    printMaybeResult(has_value); // Output: Value: 100
    printMaybeResult(no_value);  // Output: No value.
}

fn printMaybeResult(result: MaybeResult) void {
    if (result) |r| {
        switch (r) {
            .value => |v| std.debug.print("Value: {}\n", .{v}),
            .none => std.debug.print("No value.\n", .{}),
        }
    } else {
        std.debug.print("No value.\n", .{});
    }
}
```

Representing State and Choices Safely:

Enums for State: Use enums to represent a fixed set of distinct states that an object or system can be in (e.g., Loading, Ready, Error).[4]

Tagged Unions for Choices with Data: When a choice implies that the data has a specific structure or type associated with it, use tagged unions. This ensures that you know exactly what kind of data you're working with based on the tag. For example, a `Result` type that can be either a successful value (of a certain type) or an error (with error information).

Error Handling with Tagged Unions: As seen with the `OperationResult` example, tagged unions are excellent for representing the outcome of operations that can either succeed with a value or fail with an error.

In summary, enums provide a type-safe way to represent a limited set of named constants, ideal for defining states and options. Tagged unions build upon this by combining an enum with a union, allowing you to represent data that can take on different forms based on a tag. This pattern enhances type safety, code clarity, and helps prevent common errors associated with traditional unions, making them a powerful tool for representing state and choices safely in Zig.

CHAPTER 4

Memory Management in Zig: Control and Safety

4.1 Understanding Zig's Approach to Memory Allocation: Arenas and Allocators

Alright, let's delve into Zig's approach to memory allocation, focusing on the concepts of Arenas and Allocators. Understanding these is crucial for managing memory effectively in Zig, especially when aiming for performance and control.

1. The Need for Memory Management:

As you know, in Zig, memory management is manual. This means you, the programmer, are responsible for deciding when and how memory is allocated (reserved) and deallocated (freed). This control is vital for performance-critical applications where garbage collection pauses or unpredictable memory behavior are unacceptable.

2. Allocators: The Abstraction for Memory Operations:

Zig introduces the concept of **allocators** as an abstraction for how memory is managed. An allocator is an object that provides a consistent interface for allocating and deallocating blocks of memory. This abstraction offers several benefits:

Flexibility: You can use different allocator implementations tailored to specific needs (e.g., general-purpose heap, arena-based, fixed-size buffer).

Testability: You can use special allocators in testing environments to detect memory leaks and other memory-related issues.

Control: Allocators give you fine-grained control over how memory is obtained and released.

The `std.mem` module in Zig provides several built-in allocator implementations. The core interface for an allocator typically includes functions like:

`alloc(len: usize, align: u29) ?[*]u8` **(or** `alloc(T: type, count: usize, ?align: u29) ?[*]T`**):** Allocates a block of `len` bytes (or `count` elements of type `T`) with the specified alignment. Returns a pointer to the allocated memory or `null` if allocation fails.

`free(ptr: [*]u8, ?len: usize, ?align: u29) void` **(or** `free(ptr: [*]T, count: usize, ?align: u29) void`**):** Deallocates the memory pointed to by `ptr`. It's crucial to free memory using the same allocator that was used to allocate it. The `len` and `align` parameters might be optional depending on the allocator implementation, as some allocators track this information internally.

3. Arenas: A Specific Memory Allocation Strategy:

An **arena allocator** is a type of allocator that allocates memory from a contiguous block (the "arena"). The key characteristic of an arena allocator is that all allocations made from a single arena are typically freed at once when the arena itself is deinitialized. This strategy offers several advantages:

Efficiency of Deallocation: Freeing all memory allocated within an arena is very fast – it usually just involves resetting a pointer or freeing the entire underlying block. You don't need to individually track and free each allocation.

Reduced Fragmentation: Compared to general-purpose heap allocators that can suffer from memory fragmentation over time (small, scattered blocks of free memory), arena allocators tend to have less fragmentation because allocations happen sequentially within the arena.

Simplified Lifetime Management: Arenas can tie the lifetime of multiple related allocations to the lifetime of the arena itself. When the task or scope associated with the arena is finished, all its memory can be released together.

4. How Arenas Work in Zig (using `std.heap.ArenaAllocator`):

To use an arena allocator in Zig, you typically:

1.**Create an** `ArenaAllocator`**:** You need to provide an initial memory arena (a block of memory) to the `ArenaAllocator`. This arena can be obtained from another allocator (like the general-purpose allocator) or even a fixed-size buffer on the stack.

2. **Obtain an Allocator Interface:** The `ArenaAllocator` provides an `allocator()` method that returns a standard `std.mem.Allocator` interface. You use this interface to perform allocations within the arena.

3. **Perform Allocations:** Use the `alloc` method of the obtained allocator to allocate memory for your data structures.

4. **Deinitialize the Arena:** When you're done with all the memory allocated from the arena, you call the `deinit()` method of the

`ArenaAllocator`. This frees the entire underlying memory block (if it was obtained from another allocator) or resets the arena.

Code Illustration of Arena Allocation:

Code snippet

```
const std = @import("std");

pub fn processData(allocator: std.mem.Allocator) !void {
    // Allocate a slice for names
    const names = try allocator.alloc([]const u8, 3);
    defer allocator.free(names);

    names[0] = try allocator.alloc(u8, 5);
    std.mem.copy(u8, names[0], "Alice");
    defer allocator.free(names[0]);

    names[1] = try allocator.alloc(u8, 3);
    std.mem.copy(u8, names[1], "Bob");
    defer allocator.free(names[1]);

    names[2] = try allocator.alloc(u8, 5);
    std.mem.copy(u8, names[2], "Charlie");
    defer allocator.free(names[2]);

    for (names) |name| {
        std.debug.print("Name: {s}\n", .{name});
    }
}

pub fn main() !void {
    var gpa = std.heap.GeneralPurposeAllocator(.{}){};
    defer gpa.deinit();
```

```
    // Create a memory arena using the general-purpose allocator
    var arena = std.heap.ArenaAllocator.init(gpa.allocator());
    defer arena.deinit();
    const arena_allocator = arena.allocator();

    try processData(arena_allocator);

    std.debug.print("Data processing complete.\n", .{});
    // All memory allocated within the arena in processData is
automatically freed when arena.deinit() is called.
}
```

Key Concepts and Nuances:

Allocator Interface: The `std.mem.Allocator` interface provides a standard way to interact with different memory management strategies. You can pass an allocator around to functions that need to allocate memory without needing to know the underlying implementation.

Arena Lifetime: The key to using arenas effectively is to tie their lifetime to a specific scope or task. When that scope or task ends, you deinitialize the arena, freeing all associated memory.

Nested Arenas: You can even create arenas within other arenas, allowing for hierarchical memory management.

Choosing the Right Allocator:

Use `GeneralPurposeAllocator` for general heap allocations with individual allocation and deallocation.

Use `ArenaAllocator` when you have a group of related allocations that can be freed together at the end of a scope or operation. This can be more efficient and reduce fragmentation.

Other allocators like `FixedBufferAllocator` are useful for specific scenarios where you have a known, limited amount of memory.

`defer` **with Arena Allocators:** While `defer` `allocator.free(ptr)` is still valid within an arena, the primary benefit of an arena is the bulk deallocation with `defer` `arena.deinit()`. Be mindful of the lifetime of individual allocations if you're mixing these approaches.

In Summary:

Zig's approach to memory allocation centers around the concept of **allocators**, which provide an abstraction for memory operations. **Arenas** are a specific type of allocator that manages memory within a contiguous block and allows for efficient bulk deallocation. By choosing the appropriate allocator for the task and understanding the lifecycle of memory managed by arenas, you can achieve efficient and predictable memory management in your Zig applications. Arenas are particularly useful for managing temporary allocations within a specific scope or function call.

4.2 Manual Memory Management: Best Practices for Avoiding Common Pitfalls

Let's discuss best practices for manual memory management in Zig to help you avoid common pitfalls that can lead to bugs, crashes, and security vulnerabilities. Since you have explicit control over memory, it's crucial to follow these guidelines diligently.

1. Pair Every Allocation with a Deallocation:

The Golden Rule: For every call to an allocation function (e.g., `alloc`, `realloc`, `calloc` from an allocator), there must be a corresponding call to the deallocation function (`free`) on the *same* allocator.

Use `defer`: Zig's `defer` keyword is invaluable for ensuring that deallocation happens automatically when the current scope is exited, regardless of how the scope is exited (normal return, early return, or panic in debug builds).

Code snippet

```
const std = @import("std");

fn processData(allocator: std.mem.Allocator) !void {
    const buffer = try allocator.alloc(u8, 1024);
    defer allocator.free(buffer); // Guaranteed to be called when processData exits

    // Use the buffer...
    std.mem.set(u8, buffer, 0, 1024);
    std.debug.print("Buffer initialized.\n", .{});
}

pub fn main() !void {
    var gpa = std.heap.GeneralPurposeAllocator(.{}){};
    defer gpa.deinit();
    const allocator = gpa.allocator();
    try processData(allocator);
```

```
}
```

2. Free Memory Only Once:

Double Free Error: Freeing the same block of memory more than once leads to undefined behavior and can cause crashes or memory corruption.

Careful with Ownership: Be very clear about which part of your code "owns" a piece of allocated memory and is responsible for freeing it. Avoid passing ownership implicitly.

Code snippet

```
const std = @import("std");

fn allocateAndReturn(allocator: std.mem.Allocator) ![*]u8 {
    return try allocator.alloc(u8, 10);
}

pub fn main() !void {
    var gpa = std.heap.GeneralPurposeAllocator(.{}){};
    defer gpa.deinit();
    const allocator = gpa.allocator();

    const ptr = try allocateAndReturn(allocator);
    defer allocator.free(ptr); // Freeing once is correct

    // allocator.free(ptr); // This second free would be a double free
error!
```

}

3. Avoid Use-After-Free Errors:

Dangling Pointers: After freeing a block of memory, any pointers that still point to that memory become "dangling pointers." Accessing the memory through a dangling pointer leads to undefined behavior.

Set Pointers to `null`: If a pointer might be used after the memory it points to is freed, consider setting the pointer to `null` to explicitly indicate that it's no longer valid. Then, check for `null` before dereferencing.

Code snippet

```
const std = @import("std");

pub fn main() !void {
    var gpa = std.heap.GeneralPurposeAllocator(.{}){};
    defer gpa.deinit();
    const allocator = gpa.allocator();

    var ptr = try allocator.alloc(u8, 5);
    defer allocator.free(ptr);

    std.mem.copy(u8, ptr, "Hello");
    std.debug.print("Value: {s}\n", .{ptr});
```

```
allocator.free(ptr);
ptr = null; // Set to null after freeing

if (ptr != null) {
    // std.debug.print("Value after free: {s}\n", .{ptr}); // This would
likely crash or produce garbage
    } else {
    std.debug.print("Pointer is now null.\n", .{});
    }
}
```

4. Initialize Memory After Allocation:

Uninitialized Memory: Allocated memory might contain garbage data. Always initialize the memory to a known state before using it.

`std.mem.set` **and other utilities:** Use functions like `std.mem.set` to fill memory with a specific value or `std.mem.copy` to copy data into the allocated region.

Code snippet

```
const std = @import("std");

pub fn main() !void {
    var gpa = std.heap.GeneralPurposeAllocator(.{}){};
    defer gpa.deinit();
    const allocator = gpa.allocator();
```

```
    const buffer = try allocator.alloc(i32, 3);
    defer allocator.free(buffer);

    std.mem.set(i32, buffer, 0, 0); // Initialize all elements to 0
    buffer[0] = 10;
    buffer[1] = 20;
    buffer[2] = 30;

    std.debug.print("Initialized buffer: {any}\n", .{buffer});
}
```

5. Allocate Sufficient Memory:

Buffer Overflows: Ensure that the allocated buffer is large enough to hold the data you intend to store in it. Writing beyond the bounds of an allocated buffer can corrupt adjacent memory and lead to crashes or security vulnerabilities.

Careful with String Manipulation: When working with strings, always allocate enough space for the string content, including the null terminator if required by C APIs. Use functions that respect buffer boundaries (e.g., `std.mem.copy` with explicit lengths).

Code snippet

```
const std = @import("std");

pub fn main() !void {
    var gpa = std.heap.GeneralPurposeAllocator(.{}){};
    defer gpa.deinit();
```

```
    const allocator = gpa.allocator();

    const source = "This is a string.";
     const buffer = try allocator.alloc(u8, source.len + 1); // +1 for null
terminator if needed
    defer allocator.free(buffer);

    std.mem.copy(u8, buffer, source);
    buffer[source.len] = 0; // Null-terminate if interacting with C

    std.debug.print("Copied string: {s}\n", .{buffer});
}
```

6. Choose the Right Allocator for the Task:

General-Purpose: Use `std.heap.GeneralPurposeAllocator` for most general heap allocations where individual allocation and deallocation are needed.

Arena Allocators: Employ `std.heap.ArenaAllocator` for managing memory within a specific scope or operation where you can free all allocations at once. This can improve efficiency and reduce fragmentation.

Fixed-Size Buffers: Consider `std.heap.FixedBufferAllocator` for situations where you have a known, limited amount of memory available (e.g., on the stack).

Custom Allocators: Zig allows you to implement your own allocators if you have very specific memory management requirements.

7. Be Mindful of Alignment:

Data Alignment: Different data types have alignment requirements. The allocator's `alloc` function allows you to specify the alignment. Incorrect alignment can lead to performance penalties or even crashes on some architectures.

Pointer Casting: Be cautious when casting pointers to different types, especially if the target type has stricter alignment requirements than the original allocation.

Code snippet

```
const std = @import("std");

pub fn main() !void {
    var gpa = std.heap.GeneralPurposeAllocator(.{}){};
    defer gpa.deinit();
    const allocator = gpa.allocator();

    const aligned_ptr = try allocator.alloc(u64, 1, @alignOf(u64));
    defer allocator.free(aligned_ptr);
    aligned_ptr.* = 0x1234567890ABCDEF;
    std.debug.print("Aligned value: {x}\n", .{aligned_ptr.*});

    // Casting to a less aligned pointer might cause issues on some architectures
    const byte_ptr = @ptrCast([*]u8, aligned_ptr);
    byte_ptr[0] = 0xFF; // Potentially problematic if alignment is strictly enforced
```

```
    std.debug.print("Modified byte: {x}\n", .{aligned_ptr.*});
}
```

8. Use Tools for Detection:

Zig's Debug Mode: Zig's debug mode often includes checks for memory leaks and other memory-related errors. Run your code with `zig build run -Drelease=false` (or just `zig build run`) during development.

Testing with `std.testing.allocator`**:** Use the testing allocator in your unit tests to automatically track allocations and ensure that all allocated memory is freed by the end of the test.

Code snippet

```
const std = @import("std");
const testing = std.testing;

test "memory leak detection" {
    var test_allocator = testing.allocator;
    {
        _ = try test_allocator.alloc(u8, 10);
        // Forgot to free this memory!
    }
    try test_allocator.expectLeaks(); // This test will fail due to the
unfreed allocation
}
```

9. Keep Ownership Clear:

Document Ownership: Clearly document which part of your code is responsible for allocating and freeing a particular piece of memory, especially when passing pointers between functions or modules.

Avoid Global Mutable State: Global mutable memory can make it harder to track ownership and lifetimes.

10. Review and Test Thoroughly:

Code Reviews: Have your code reviewed by others to catch potential memory management issues.

Comprehensive Testing: Write thorough unit and integration tests that exercise different memory allocation and deallocation scenarios.

By adhering to these best practices, you can significantly reduce the risk of common pitfalls associated with manual memory management in Zig and build more reliable and robust applications. Remember that vigilance and careful attention to detail are key.

4.3 Leveraging Built-in Memory Safety Features and Tools

Alright, let's explore how Zig helps you maintain memory safety through its built-in language features and tools, even while providing manual memory management. These features aim to catch common memory errors at compile time or during development, reducing the risk of runtime crashes and security vulnerabilities.[1]

1. No Implicit Pointer Dereferencing:

Explicitness: Unlike some languages where pointer dereferencing can happen implicitly, in Zig, you must explicitly dereference a pointer using the .* operator.[2] This makes it clear when you are accessing the value pointed to by a pointer, reducing the chance of accidentally using an invalid pointer.

Code snippet

```
const std = @import("std");

pub fn main() !void {
    var x: i32 = 10;
    const ptr: *i32 = &x;

    std.debug.print("Value: {}\n", .{ptr.*}); // Explicit dereference

    // std.debug.print("Value: {}\n", .{ptr}); // This would print the
memory address
}
```

2. Optional Types (?T) for Null Safety:

Explicit Nullability: Zig's optional types (?T) explicitly indicate when a value might be absent (similar to null in other languages). You cannot directly access the underlying value of an optional type without first checking if it's present. This helps prevent null pointer exceptions.

Code snippet

```zig
const std = @import("std");

fn findUser(id: u32) ?[]const u8 {
    if (id == 1) {
        return "Alice";
    } else {
        return null;
    }
}

pub fn main() !void {
    const user1 = findUser(1);
    if (user1) |name| {
        std.debug.print("User found: {s}\n", .{name});
    } else {
        std.debug.print("User not found.\n", .{});
    }

    const user2 = findUser(2);
    if (user2) |name| {
        std.debug.print("User found: {s}\n", .{name});
    } else {
        std.debug.print("User not found.\n", .{});
    }

    // std.debug.print("User 1 name: {s}\n", .{user1.?}); // Direct access to optional value using .? (only safe if you know it's not null)
}
```

3. Error Unions (!T) for Explicit Error Handling:

Checked Exceptions: Zig's error unions force you to explicitly handle potential errors returned by functions.[3] The `try` keyword makes it clear where errors might occur, and `catch` blocks ensure that these errors are dealt with. This reduces the likelihood of unhandled exceptions leading to crashes.

Code snippet

```
const std = @import("std");
const fs = std.fs;

pub fn readFile(path: []const u8) ![]u8 {
    const file = try fs.openFile(path, .{}) catch |err| return err;
    defer file.close();
    const contents = try file.readToEndAlloc(std.heap.page_allocator);
    return contents;
}

pub fn main() !void {
    const result = readFile("my_file.txt") catch |err| {
        std.debug.print("Error reading file: {}\n", .{err});
        return;
    };

    if (result) |contents| {
        std.debug.print("File contents: {s}\n", .{contents});
        std.heap.page_allocator.free(contents);
    }
}
```

4. Bounds Checking (in Debug Builds):

Array and Slice Access: In debug builds, Zig automatically performs bounds checking on array and slice accesses. If you try to access an element outside the valid range, a panic (controlled crash with an error message) will occur, helping you identify and fix out-of-bounds errors during development. This can be disabled in release builds for performance.

Code snippet

```
const std = @import("std");

pub fn main() !void {
    const numbers = [_]i32{10, 20, 30};
    std.debug.print("Element 0: {}\n", .{numbers[0]}); // Safe access
    // std.debug.print("Element 3: {}\n", .{numbers[3]}); // This will
panic in debug mode
}
```

5. Memory Safety Checks in Testing:

`std.testing.allocator`: The built-in testing framework provides a special allocator (`std.testing.allocator`) that tracks all allocations made during a test. At the end of the test, it can check if any memory was leaked (allocated but not freed), causing the test to fail. This is a powerful tool for ensuring that your memory management is correct.

Code snippet

```
const std = @import("std");
const testing = std.testing;

test "no memory leaks in data processing" {
    var test_allocator = testing.allocator;
    {
        try processData(test_allocator);
    }
    try test_allocator.expectLeaks();
}

fn processData(allocator: std.mem.Allocator) !void {
    const buffer = try allocator.alloc(u8, 10);
    defer allocator.free(buffer);
    std.mem.set(u8, buffer, 0, 10);
}
```

6. No Implicit Type Conversions (Especially Pointers):

Explicitness: Zig requires explicit type casts using @ptrCast, @intCast, etc. This prevents accidental misinterpretations of data types, especially when dealing with pointers where casting to an incompatible type can lead to memory corruption.

Code snippet

```
const std = @import("std");

pub fn main() !void {
    var x: u32 = 0x12345678;
    const ptr_u32: *u32 = &x;
    const ptr_u8: *u8 = @ptrCast(*u8, ptr_u32); // Explicit cast

    std.debug.print("u32 value: {x}\n", .{ptr_u32.*});
    std.debug.print("First byte (as u8): {x}\n", .{ptr_u8.*});
}
```

7. Compile-Time Safety Checks (`comptime`):

Early Error Detection: Zig's compile-time execution (`comptime`) allows you to perform certain checks and computations at compile time.[4] This can catch potential errors related to memory layout, sizes, and other invariants before your program even runs.

Code snippet

```
const std = @import("std");

const SIZE: comptime usize = 10;

pub fn main() !void {
    var array: [SIZE]i32 = undefined;
    // comptime {
```

```
//    if (SIZE > 100) {
//        @compileError("Array size is too large!");
//    }
// }

    for (0..SIZE) |i| {
        array[i] = @intCast(i32, i);
    }
    std.debug.print("Array: {any}\n", .{array});
}
```

8. Built-in Functions for Memory Operations:

Safe Utilities: The std.mem module provides functions like copy, set, zero_init, etc., which are designed to be safer than manual byte-level manipulations. They often take sizes explicitly, reducing the risk of buffer overflows if used correctly.

Code snippet

```
const std = @import("std");

pub fn main() !void {
    var gpa = std.heap.GeneralPurposeAllocator(.{}){};
    defer gpa.deinit();
    const allocator = gpa.allocator();

    const dest = try allocator.alloc(u8, 10);
    defer allocator.free(dest);
    const src = "Hello";
```

```
std.mem.copy(u8, dest, src); // Safe copy with explicit length
std.debug.print("Copied: {s}\n", .{dest});
}
```

How to Leverage These Features:

Embrace Explicitness: Zig's design encourages you to be explicit in your code.[5] Take advantage of this by using optional types, handling errors with `try` and `catch`, and performing explicit type casts.

Test Thoroughly: Utilize the built-in testing framework and the `std.testing.allocator` to catch memory leaks and other issues.[6]

Run in Debug Mode: Develop and test your code frequently in debug mode to benefit from bounds checking and other runtime safety checks.[7]

Use Standard Library Functions: Leverage the safe memory manipulation utilities provided in `std.mem`.

Understand `comptime`: Explore how compile-time execution can help you enforce invariants and catch errors early.

By understanding and actively using these built-in memory safety features and tools, you can write more robust and reliable Zig code, even with manual memory management. Zig aims to provide a safer low-level programming experience compared to languages like C and C++.

CHAPTER 5

Error Handling: Robustness in High-Performance Systems

5.1 The error Type and Error Sets: A Practical Approach to Error Handling

Alright, let's dive into Zig's approach to error handling, focusing on the `error` type and error sets. This is a fundamental aspect of writing robust and reliable software in Zig, as it emphasizes explicit error handling without relying on exceptions.

1. The `error` Builtin Type:

In Zig, `error` is a builtin type that represents a set of possible error values. Unlike exceptions in other languages, errors in Zig are just values. This means they can be returned from functions, stored in variables, and explicitly checked.

Defining Error Sets: You define a set of named error values using the `error` keyword followed by a block `{}` containing the error names (identifiers). These names are like constants of the `error` type.

Code snippet

```
const std = @import("std");

const FileError = error {
    FileNotFound,
    PermissionDenied,
```

```
    DiskFull,
};

const NetworkError = error {
    ConnectionFailed,
    Timeout,
    InvalidResponse,
};

pub fn main() !void {
    const file_not_found: FileError = .FileNotFound;
    const connection_failed: NetworkError = .ConnectionFailed;

    std.debug.print("File error: {}\n", .{file_not_found});
    std.debug.print("Network error: {}\n", .{connection_failed});

    if (file_not_found == .FileNotFound) {
        std.debug.print("The file was not found.\n", .{});
    }
}
```

Combining Error Sets (Error Unions): Functions that can fail will typically return an **error union** type. This is denoted by a ! before the return type (e.g., ! [ ] u8 means the function can return either a [ ]u8 or an error from an implicitly combined error set). The compiler automatically unions all the potential error sets that can be returned within the function.

Code snippet

```zig
const std = @import("std");
const fs = std.fs;

fn readFile(path: []const u8) ![]u8 {
    const file = try fs.openFile(path, .{}) catch |err| return err;
    defer file.close();
    const            contents       =       try
file.readToEndAlloc(std.heap.page_allocator);
    return contents;
}


pub fn main() !void {
    const result = readFile("non_existent_file.txt") catch |err| {
        std.debug.print("Error: {}\n", .{err});
        return;
    };

    if (result) |contents| {
        std.debug.print("File contents: {s}\n", .{contents});
        std.heap.page_allocator.free(contents);
    }
}
```

In readFile, fs.openFile can return errors from std.fs.Error, and file.readToEndAlloc can return errors from std.io.Error (which might include OutOfMemory). The ! return type implicitly represents the union of all these potential errors.

2. Handling Errors with try and catch:

try **Keyword:** When you call a function that returns an error union, you use the try keyword. If the function returns a success value, `try` unwraps that value. If the function returns an error, the execution immediately jumps to the nearest enclosing `catch` block.

`catch` **Block:** The `catch` block allows you to handle the error. You can optionally specify a variable name after `catch` (e.g., `catch |err|`) to capture the error value.

Code snippet

```
const std = @import("std");
const fs = std.fs;

pub fn main() !void {
    const result = readFile("config.txt") catch |err| {
        std.debug.print("Failed to read config: {}\n", .{err});
        return; // Exit the main function on error
    };

    if (result) |contents| {
        std.debug.print("Config contents:\n{s}\n", .{contents});
        std.heap.page_allocator.free(contents);
    }
}

fn readFile(path: []const u8) ![]u8 {
    const file = try fs.openFile(path, .{}) catch |err| return err;
    defer file.close();
    const contents = try file.readToEndAlloc(std.heap.page_allocator);
    return contents;
}
```

catch with Specific Errors: You can also use `catch` with a specific error set or error value to handle only certain types of errors.

Code snippet

```
const std = @import("std");
const fs = std.fs;
const builtin = @import("builtin");

fn readFile(path: []const u8) ![]u8 {
    const file = try fs.openFile(path, .{}) catch |err| switch (err) {
        error.FileNotFound => {
            std.debug.print("File not found: {}\n", .{path});
            return err;
        },
        error.PermissionDenied => {
            std.debug.print("Permission denied for: {}\n", .{path});
            return err;
        },
        else => {
            std.debug.print("Error opening file: {}\n", .{err});
            return err;
        },
    };
    defer file.close();
    const contents = try file.readToEndAlloc(std.heap.page_allocator);
    return contents;
```

```
}

pub fn main() !void {
    _ = readFile("protected_file.txt") catch unreachable;
}
```

The `switch (err)` within the `catch` block allows you to handle different error cases specifically. The `else` case acts as a catch-all for other errors.

`catch unreachable`: If you are certain that a `try` expression will never return an error (e.g., based on compile-time knowledge), you can use `catch unreachable`. If an error does occur, it will trigger a panic in debug builds.

3. Error Propagation:

A common pattern in Zig is to propagate errors up the call stack. If a function encounters an error that it cannot handle, it often returns that error to its caller. The caller can then decide how to handle the error (e.g., retry the operation, return a different error, or terminate the program).

Code snippet

```
const std = @import("std");
const fs = std.fs;

fn loadConfig(path: []const u8) ![]u8 {
    const contents = try readFile(path); // Propagate the error from
readFile
    return contents;
```

```
}

pub fn main() !void {
    const config = loadConfig("app.config") catch |err| {
        std.debug.print("Failed to load configuration: {}\n", .{err});
        return;
    };

    if (config) |c| {
        std.debug.print("Config loaded successfully:\n{s}\n", .{c});
        std.heap.page_allocator.free(c);
    }
}

fn readFile(path: []const u8) ![]u8 {
    const file = try fs.openFile(path, .{}) catch |err| return err;
    defer file.close();
                        const        contents     =        try
file.readToEndAlloc(std.heap.page_allocator);
    return contents;
}
```

In `loadConfig`, if `readFile` returns an error, `loadConfig` simply returns that error. The `main` function then catches and handles the error.

4. Practical Approach to Error Handling:

Define Meaningful Error Sets: Create error sets that clearly describe the possible failure modes of your functions or modules. This makes error handling more informative.

Return Error Unions: For functions that can fail, use the ! return type to indicate that they can return either a success value or an error.

Handle Errors Explicitly: Use `try` to call fallible functions and `catch` to handle the errors. Don't ignore errors.

Propagate When Necessary: If a function cannot meaningfully handle an error, propagate it to the caller.

Use `switch` for Detailed Error Handling: When you need to handle different error cases in a specific way, use a `switch` statement on the error value within a `catch` block.

Consider `catch unreachable` Carefully: Only use `catch unreachable` when you have a strong compile-time guarantee that an error will not occur. Misuse can hide bugs.

Avoid Excessive Nesting: Deeply nested `try...catch` blocks can make code harder to read. Consider breaking down complex operations into smaller functions.

Document Errors: Clearly document the possible errors that a function can return.

Benefits of Zig's Error Handling:

Explicitness: Error handling is a visible part of the code through the `!` return type and `try`/`catch` keywords. This makes it harder to ignore potential failures.

No Hidden Control Flow: Unlike exceptions, error returns and `catch` blocks create explicit control flow, making it easier to reason about the program's execution.

Performance: Error returns are typically more performant than exception handling mechanisms in many other languages.

Clarity: Error sets provide a clear and concise way to define and categorize errors.

By embracing Zig's approach to error handling with the `error` type and error sets, you can write more robust, maintainable, and performant software by explicitly managing potential failures.

5.2 Recoverable and Unrecoverable Errors: Strategies for Different Scenarios

Alright, let's discuss how Zig distinguishes between recoverable and unrecoverable errors and explore strategies for handling each scenario effectively. This distinction is crucial for building robust applications that can gracefully handle failures when possible and terminate safely when necessary.[1]

1. Recoverable Errors:

Recoverable errors are situations that your program can potentially handle and continue execution, possibly after taking some corrective action or informing the user.[2] These are the types of errors that Zig's error unions and `try/catch` mechanism are primarily designed for.

Examples of Recoverable Errors:

File not found. The program might prompt the user for a different file or use a default configuration.

Network timeout. The program might retry the connection or inform the user about the network issue.

Invalid user input. The program might ask the user to re-enter the data.

Resource temporarily unavailable (e.g., a database connection pool is exhausted). The program might wait and retry.

Strategies for Handling Recoverable Errors:

Catch and Handle: Use `try` to call the fallible operation and `catch` to handle the specific error. Within the `catch` block, you can implement logic to recover from the error.

Code snippet

```
const std = @import("std");
const fs = std.fs;

fn loadConfiguration(path: []const u8) ![]u8 {
    const file = try fs.openFile(path, .{}) catch |err| {
        if (err == error.FileNotFound) {
            std.debug.print("Configuration file not found. Using default settings.\n", .{});
                return  try  std.mem.dupe(std.heap.page_allocator, "default_config");
        } else {
            return err; // Propagate other errors
        }
    };
    defer file.close();
    return try file.readToEndAlloc(std.heap.page_allocator);
}

pub fn main() !void {
```

```
const config = loadConfiguration("app.config") catch |err| {
    std.debug.print("Failed to load configuration: {}\n", .{err});
    return;
};

if (config) |c| {
    std.debug.print("Configuration: {s}\n", .{c});
    std.heap.page_allocator.free(c);
}
}
```

Retry: For transient errors (like network issues), you might implement a retry mechanism with a limited number of attempts or an exponential backoff strategy.

Code snippet

```
const std = @import("std");
const time = std.time;

fn fetchDataWithRetry(url: []const u8, max_retries: u32) ![]u8 {
    var attempts: u32 = 0;
    while (attempts < max_retries) {
        const result = fetchData(url);
        if (result) |data| return data;
        else |err| {
```

```
            std.debug.print("Fetch failed (attempt {}): {}\n", .{attempts +
1, err});
        attempts += 1;
                    time.sleep(time.milliseconds(100 << attempts));  //
Exponential backoff
    }
  }
  return error.NetworkError; // Return error if all retries fail
}


fn fetchData(url: []const u8) ![]u8 {
  // Simulate network request that might fail

                                                                    if
(std.rand.DefaultPrng.init(time.nanoTimestamp()).random().float(f3
2) < 0.5) {
      return "Data from network";
  } else {
      return error.NetworkError;
  }
}


pub fn main() !void {
    const data = fetchDataWithRetry("example.com/data", 3) catch
|err| {
        std.debug.print("Failed to fetch data after multiple retries:
{}\n", .{err});
      return;
  };

  std.debug.print("Successfully fetched data: {s}\n", .{data});
  std.heap.page_allocator.free(data);
}
```

Provide Alternatives or Defaults: If an operation fails, you might be able to use a default value or a fallback mechanism to continue.

Inform the User: For user-facing applications, it's important to provide informative error messages to the user and guide them on how to resolve the issue.

2. Unrecoverable Errors:

Unrecoverable errors are critical situations where the program cannot continue to function safely or correctly. In these cases, the best course of action is usually to terminate the program to prevent further damage or unpredictable behavior.

Examples of Unrecoverable Errors:

Out of memory (when the program cannot function without more memory).

Data corruption that makes further processing unreliable.

Violation of critical invariants or assumptions within the program's logic.

Failure to initialize essential system resources.

Security vulnerabilities detected at runtime.

Strategies for Handling Unrecoverable Errors:

Panic: Zig's `panic()` function is the standard way to indicate an unrecoverable error. When `panic()` is called, the program will typically print an error message (including stack trace in debug builds) and terminate.

Code snippet

```
const std = @import("std");

fn initializeCriticalResource() !*opaque {
    // Simulate resource initialization that might fail
    if (std.rand.DefaultPrng.init(std.time.nanoTimestamp()).random().float(f32) < 0.2) {
        return @ptrCast(*opaque, try std.heap.page_allocator.alloc(u8, 10));
    } else {
        return error.ResourceInitializationFailed;
    }
}

pub fn main() !void {
    const resource = initializeCriticalResource() catch |err| {
        std.debug.print("Failed to initialize critical resource: {}\n", .{err});
        std.panic("Could not start the application due to resource initialization failure.");
    };
    defer std.heap.page_allocator.free(@ptrCast([*]u8, resource));
```

```zig
    std.debug.print("Application started successfully.\n", .{});
    // ... rest of the application logic ...
}
```

Logging and Termination: Before panicking, it's often a good idea to log the error details to a file or system log to aid in debugging.

Cleanup Before Termination: Use `defer` statements to ensure that essential cleanup operations (like freeing allocated memory or closing files) are performed before the program terminates due to a panic.[3]

Returning Error from `main()`: While `panic()` is typical for unrecoverable errors within the application's core logic, if a critical error occurs during the very initial setup in `main()`, you can also return an error from `main()`. The Zig runtime environment will typically handle this by exiting with a non-zero exit code.

Code snippet

```zig
const std = @import("std");
```

```
pub fn main() !void {
    if (checkEnvironmentVariables()) {
        std.debug.print("Environment checks passed.\n", .{});
        // ... rest of the application ...
        return;
    } else {
        std.debug.print("Critical environment variables not set.\n", .{});
        return error.EnvironmentError;
    }
}


fn checkEnvironmentVariables() bool {
    // Simulate checking for required environment variables
    return std.os.getenv("API_KEY") != null and
        std.os.getenv("DATABASE_URL") != null;
}
```

Key Considerations:

Clarity of Error Semantics: Clearly define which errors in your system are considered recoverable and which are unrecoverable. This helps in making consistent error handling decisions.

Context Matters: Whether an error is recoverable or unrecoverable can depend on the context of the operation and the overall state of the application.

Avoid Panicking for Recoverable Errors: Panicking should generally be reserved for situations where continued execution is unsafe or impossible. Use error unions and `try/catch` for anticipated and potentially resolvable issues.

Test Error Handling: Thoroughly test both successful execution paths and various error scenarios (both recoverable and unrecoverable) to ensure your application behaves as expected.

By carefully considering the nature of potential errors and applying appropriate strategies for recoverable and unrecoverable situations, you can build more resilient and user-friendly Zig applications. The language's explicit error handling mechanisms encourage a proactive approach to dealing with failures.

5.3 Implementing Effective Error Propagation and Handling Techniques

Alright, let's delve into implementing effective error propagation and handling techniques in Zig. This is crucial for building robust applications where errors are managed gracefully as they occur across different parts of the codebase.

1. Returning Error Unions:

The foundation of effective error propagation in Zig is using error unions ($!T$) as the return type of functions that can fail. This clearly signals to the caller that the function might return an error.

Code snippet

```
const std = @import("std");
const fs = std.fs;

fn readFile(path: []const u8) ![]u8 {
    const file = try fs.openFile(path, .{}) catch |err| return err;
    defer file.close();
```

```zig
    const contents = try file.readToEndAlloc(std.heap.page_allocator);
    return contents;
}

fn processFile(path: []const u8) !void {
    const contents = try readFile(path); // Propagates error from readFile
    defer std.heap.page_allocator.free(contents);

    // Process the file contents...
    std.debug.print("Processing file: {s}\n", .{contents});
}

pub fn main() !void {
    try processFile("data.txt"); // Handles error if processFile or readFile fails
    std.debug.print("File processed successfully.\n", .{});
}
```

In this example, both `readFile` and `processFile` can return errors. `processFile` uses `try readFile()` to propagate any error returned by `readFile` up to its caller (`main`). `main` then uses `try processFile()` to handle any potential error in the entire process.

2. The `try` Keyword for Concise Propagation:

The `try` keyword is essential for simplifying error propagation. When used with a function call that returns an error union, `try` does the following:

Success: If the function returns a success value, `try` unwraps and returns that value.

Error: If the function returns an error, `try` immediately returns that error from the current function.

This avoids the need for verbose `if (result == .err) return result;` checks after every fallible function call.

3. Handling Errors at the Appropriate Level:

Decide where it makes the most sense to handle an error. A function should typically handle errors that it can meaningfully recover from or provide more context to. Errors that cannot be handled locally should be propagated up the call stack.

Lower-Level Functions: Might catch specific errors to provide more detailed error information or attempt a local recovery (e.g., retrying a network request).

Higher-Level Functions: Often make decisions about how to respond to errors from lower levels (e.g., logging the error, informing the user, using a default value, or terminating a specific operation).

The `main` Function: Usually acts as the top-level error handler for the application. Unhandled errors reaching `main` might lead to program termination.

4. Adding Context to Errors:

When propagating errors, it's often helpful to add context to make debugging easier. You can achieve this by:

Returning a New Error with More Information: Catch a lower-level error and return a new error from the current function that includes details about the operation that failed.

Code snippet

```
const std = @import("std");
const fs = std.fs;

const ConfigError = error {
    FileNotFound,
    InvalidFormat,
    ReadError,
};

fn loadRawConfig(path: []const u8) ![]u8 {
    return fs.readFileAlloc(std.heap.page_allocator, path) catch |err|
{
        if (err == error.FileNotFound) {
            return ConfigError.FileNotFound;
        } else {
            std.debug.print("Low-level file read error: {}\n", .{err});
            return ConfigError.ReadError;
        }
    };
}

fn parseConfig(raw: []const u8) !std.json.Value {
    // Simulate JSON parsing that might fail
    const result = std.json.parse(raw, .{});
    if (result) |json| return json;
    else return ConfigError.InvalidFormat;
}

fn loadAppConfig(path: []const u8) !std.json.Value {
    const raw_config = try loadRawConfig(path);
    defer std.heap.page_allocator.free(raw_config);
    return try parseConfig(raw_config);
```

```
}

pub fn main() !void {
    const config = loadAppConfig("app_config.json") catch |err| {
        std.debug.print("Error loading application config: {}\n", .{err});
        return;
    };

    if (config) |c| {
        std.debug.print("App config: {}\n", .{c});
        c.deinit();
    }
}
```

Here, `loadRawConfig` catches `error.FileNotFound` and returns `ConfigError.FileNotFound`, providing more application-specific context. Other file system errors are wrapped in `ConfigError.ReadError` after logging the low-level error.

Including Additional Information in Error Handling: The `catch` `|err|` syntax allows you to access the original error value and potentially include it in logging or user-facing messages.

5. Using `switch` **for Detailed Error Handling:**

When a function can return multiple specific errors, using a `switch` statement within a `catch` block allows you to handle each error case differently.

Code snippet

```
const std = @import("std");
```

```
const os = std.os;

fn checkFilePermissions(path: []const u8) !void {
    const info = try os.stat(path) catch |err| return err;
    if (!info.mode.user.read) {
        return error.PermissionDenied;
    }
}


fn backupFile(source: []const u8, destination: []const u8) !void {
    try os.copyFile(source, destination) catch |err| switch (err) {
        error.FileNotFound => std.debug.print("Source file not found: {s}\n", .{source}),
        error.PermissionDenied => std.debug.print("Permission denied to access or write files.\n", .{}),
        else => std.debug.print("Error during backup: {}\n", .{err}),
    };
    std.debug.print("File backed up successfully from {s} to {s}.\n", .{source, destination});
}

pub fn main() !void {
    try checkFilePermissions("important.txt");
    try backupFile("important.txt", "important.bak");
}
```

In `backupFile`, the `catch` block uses a `switch` statement to provide specific messages for `error.FileNotFound` and `error.PermissionDenied`, while a general message is used for other errors.

6. Error Sets for Categorization:

Using distinct error sets (like `FileError`, `NetworkError`, `ConfigError` in the examples) helps categorize errors logically within your application. This can make error handling and debugging more organized.

7. Consider Using Result-Like Structures (When Necessary):

While Zig's error unions are powerful, in some complex scenarios, you might consider defining a custom `Result` struct or enum/union to explicitly represent either a success value or an error with associated data. This can be useful when you need to attach additional information to both success and failure outcomes. However, for most common cases, error unions are sufficient and more idiomatic.

Code snippet

```
const std = @import("std");

const Result(T) = struct {
    ok: bool,
    value: ?T = null,
    err: ?error = null,

    pub fn success(value: T) Result(T) {
        return .{ .ok = true, .value = value, .err = null };
    }

    pub fn failure(err: error) Result(T) {
        return .{ .ok = false, .value = null, .err = err };
    }

    pub fn expect(self: *const Self, message: []const u8) T {
        if (self.ok) {
            return self.value.?;
        } else {
```

```
            std.panic("{s}: {any}", .{message, self.err.?});
        }
    }
};

fn divide(a: f32, b: f32) Result(f32) {
    if (b == 0) {
        return Result(f32).failure(error.DivisionByZero);
    } else {
        return Result(f32).success(a / b);
    }
}

pub fn main() !void {
    const result1 = divide(10, 2);
        std.debug.print("Result  1:  {}\n",  .{result1.expect("Division
failed")});

    const result2 = divide(5, 0);
    if (!result2.ok) {
        std.debug.print("Error: {}\n", .{result2.err.?});
    }
}
```

Best Practices for Effective Error Handling:

Be Explicit: Always handle errors explicitly using `try` and `catch`. Don't ignore potential failures.

Provide Context: When propagating errors, add relevant context to aid in debugging.

Handle at the Right Level: Handle errors where you can meaningfully recover or provide better information. Propagate otherwise.

Use Specific Error Sets: Define error sets to categorize and provide clarity to error conditions.

Be Consistent: Adopt a consistent error handling strategy throughout your codebase.

Test Error Paths: Thoroughly test how your application handles various error scenarios.

Log Errors: Log errors, especially at higher levels, for monitoring and debugging purposes.

By following these techniques, you can implement effective error propagation and handling in Zig, leading to more reliable and maintainable applications. Zig's design encourages a proactive and explicit approach to dealing with errors.

CHAPTER 6

Concurrency and Asynchronicity: Building Responsive Applications

6.1 Exploring Zig's Concurrency Model: Goroutines and Channels (or equivalent constructs)

Alright, let's explore Zig's concurrency model. While Zig doesn't have direct equivalents to Go's "goroutines" and "channels" in the same syntactic form, it provides the fundamental building blocks and standard library support to achieve similar concurrency patterns with a strong emphasis on explicitness and control.

1. Threads as the Primary Concurrency Primitive:

Zig's concurrency model is primarily based on **threads**. The standard library (`std.Thread`) provides the necessary tools to create and manage threads.

Creating Threads: You can create a new thread by using `std.Thread.spawn`. This function takes a function pointer as an argument, which will be the entry point of the new thread.

Code snippet

```
const std = @import("std");
const time = std.time;

fn workerThread(arg: any) void {
    const id = @intCast(i32, arg);
```

```
    std.debug.print("Worker thread {} started.\n", .{id});
    time.sleep(time.milliseconds(id * 500));
    std.debug.print("Worker thread {} finished.\n", .{id});
}

pub fn main() !void {
    var threads: [3]?std.Thread = undefined;

    for (0..threads.len) |i| {
        threads[i] = try std.Thread.spawn(.{}, workerThread,
@intCast(usize, i + 1));
    }

    // Wait for all threads to finish
    for (threads) |thread_opt| {
        if (thread_opt) |thread| {
            thread.join();
        }
    }

    std.debug.print("All worker threads have completed.\n", .{});
}
```

In this example, we spawn three worker threads, each executing the `workerThread` function with a different ID as an argument. We then use `thread.join()` to wait for each thread to complete before the main function exits.

Thread Local Storage: Zig provides `std.Thread.LocalStorage` for managing data that is specific to each thread.

2. Achieving "Goroutine-like" Concurrency:

While Zig doesn't have the lightweight spawning of goroutines managed by a runtime scheduler, you can achieve a similar style of concurrent execution using threads. However, you have more explicit control over thread creation and management.

Lightweight Thread Pools (Community Libraries): For more efficient management of a large number of concurrent tasks, you might rely on community-developed libraries that implement thread pools. These libraries handle the creation and reuse of threads, which can be more performant than spawning a new OS thread for every short-lived task.

Async/Await (Experimental): Zig is actively developing an `async`/`await` feature, which will provide a more direct equivalent to lightweight concurrency similar to goroutines. This feature is not yet stable but promises to simplify asynchronous and concurrent programming without the direct overhead of OS threads for every task.

3. Communication Between Concurrent Tasks (Equivalent to Channels):

Go's channels provide a safe and convenient way for goroutines to communicate and synchronize. Zig offers several mechanisms to achieve similar inter-thread communication, though they require more explicit handling of synchronization primitives.

Atomic Operations (`std.atomic`): For simple data sharing and synchronization of basic types, Zig provides atomic operations. These operations guarantee that reads and writes to shared variables are indivisible and prevent race conditions.

Code snippet

```
const std = @import("std");
const time = std.time;
const atomic = std.atomic;

var counter: atomic.Usize = .{ .value = 0 };

fn incrementer(id: i32) void {
    for (0..10000) |_| {
        atomic.add(counter, 1, .OrderRelaxed);
    }
    std.debug.print("Incrementer {} finished.\n", .{id});
}

pub fn main() !void {
    var threads: [2]?std.Thread = undefined;

    for (0..threads.len) |i| {
        threads[i] = try std.Thread.spawn(.{}, incrementer,
@intCast(usize, i + 1));
    }

    for (threads) |thread_opt| {
        if (thread_opt) |thread| {
            thread.join();
        }
    }

    std.debug.print("Final counter value: {}\n", .{atomic.load(counter,
.OrderRelaxed)});
}
```

Mutexes (`std.Mutex`): For protecting access to shared mutable data from multiple threads, Zig provides mutexes. A mutex allows only one thread to hold a lock at a time, preventing race conditions.

Code snippet

```
const std = @import("std");
const time = std.time;
const Mutex = std.Mutex;

var shared_data: i32 = 0;
var data_mutex = Mutex.init();

fn modifyData(id: i32) void {
    data_mutex.lock();
    defer data_mutex.unlock();
    shared_data += id;
        std.debug.print("Thread {} modified data to: {}\n", .{id,
shared_data});
    time.sleep(time.milliseconds(100));
}

pub fn main() !void {
    var threads: [3]?std.Thread = undefined;

    for (0..threads.len) |i| {
            threads[i] = try std.Thread.spawn(.{}, modifyData,
@intCast(usize, i + 1));
    }
```

```zig
    for (threads) |thread_opt| {
        if (thread_opt) |thread| {
            thread.join();
        }
    }

    std.debug.print("Final shared data value: {}\n", .{shared_data});
}
```

Condition Variables (`std.Condition`): Condition variables are often used in conjunction with mutexes to allow threads to wait for a specific condition to become true.

Channels (Implemented Manually or via Libraries): Zig's standard library doesn't provide a direct "channel" type like Go's. However, you can implement channel-like behavior using combinations of mutexes, condition variables, and shared data structures (like queues or buffers).

Code snippet

```zig
const std = @import("std");
const Mutex = std.Mutex;
const Condition = std.Condition;
const ArrayList = std.ArrayList;

const Channel(T) = struct {
    mutex: Mutex = .{},
    condition: Condition = .{},
```

```
    queue: ArrayList(T),

    pub fn init(allocator: std.mem.Allocator) Channel(T) {
        return .{ .queue = ArrayList(T).init(allocator) };
    }

    pub fn deinit(self: *Self) void {
        self.queue.deinit();
    }

    pub fn send(self: *Self, value: T) !void {
        self.mutex.lock();
        defer self.mutex.unlock();
        try self.queue.append(value);
        self.condition.signal();
    }

    pub fn recv(self: *Self) !T {
        self.mutex.lock();
        defer self.mutex.unlock();
        while (self.queue.items.len == 0) {
            self.condition.wait(self.mutex);
        }
        return self.queue.pop();
    }
};

fn sender(channel: *Channel(i32)) !void {
    for (1..6) |i| {
        std.debug.print("Sending: {}\n", .{i});
        try channel.send(i);
        std.time.sleep(std.time.milliseconds(200));
    }
}
```

```
fn receiver(channel: *Channel(i32)) !void {
    for (0..5) |_| {
        const value = try channel.recv();
        std.debug.print("Received: {}\n", .{value});
    }
}

pub fn main() !void {
    var gpa = std.heap.GeneralPurposeAllocator(.{}){};
    defer gpa.deinit();
    const allocator = gpa.allocator();

    var channel = Channel(i32).init(allocator);
    defer channel.deinit();

    var sender_thread = try std.Thread.spawn(.{}, sender,
&channel);
    defer sender_thread.join();
    var receiver_thread = try std.Thread.spawn(.{}, receiver,
&channel);
    defer receiver_thread.join();
}
```

This example demonstrates a basic implementation of a channel using a mutex, condition variable, and an ArrayList. You can find more sophisticated channel implementations in community libraries.

Key Differences and Considerations:

Explicit Thread Management: Zig requires more explicit handling of thread creation and joining compared to Go's lightweight goroutines managed by a runtime.

Manual Synchronization: While Go's channels provide built-in synchronization, in Zig, you often need to use explicit synchronization primitives like mutexes, atomics, and condition variables.

No Built-in Scheduler: Zig doesn't have a built-in runtime scheduler like Go. Thread scheduling is handled by the operating system.

Focus on Control: Zig's approach prioritizes explicitness and gives you more direct control over concurrency primitives, which can be beneficial for performance-critical applications but might require more boilerplate for simpler concurrent tasks.

Async/Await Evolution: The upcoming `async/await` feature will likely bridge the gap and provide a more ergonomic way to write concurrent and asynchronous code in Zig.

In summary, while Zig doesn't have direct syntactic equivalents to goroutines and channels, it provides the fundamental building blocks (threads, atomics, mutexes, condition variables) and the standard library support to achieve similar concurrency patterns. You have more explicit control over thread management and synchronization. The ongoing development of `async/await` promises to offer a higher-level abstraction for concurrent programming in the future.

6.2 Achieving Asynchronicity with async and await (if applicable in Zig's ecosystem)

You're spot on to inquire about `async` and `await` in Zig's ecosystem! As of my last knowledge update (which is prior to this interaction), **Zig is actively developing an** `async/await` **feature,**

but it is not yet stable or part of the official language in a production-ready state.
However, there's significant ongoing work in this area, and it's a highly anticipated feature that will drastically improve how asynchronicity can be achieved in Zig.

Here's what we know and can infer about how `async`/`await` is likely to work in Zig, based on the design discussions and experimental implementations:

Likely Concepts and How They Might Work:

`async` **Functions:**

Functions marked with the `async` keyword will likely transform into state machines.

When an `await` point is reached within an `async` function, the function will suspend its execution, yielding control back to an event loop or executor.

The function will retain its state, allowing it to resume execution from the `await` point when the awaited operation completes.

`async` functions will likely return a special type representing a future or a promise (something that will eventually produce a result).

1. `await` **Keyword:**

The `await` keyword will be used within `async` functions to pause execution until the result of an asynchronous operation (a future) becomes available.

The `await` expression will likely evaluate to the result of the awaited future.

`await` will only be allowed within `async` functions.

2. Executors and Event Loops:

To actually run `async` functions and manage the suspension and resumption of tasks, Zig will likely need an executor or an event loop.

The standard library might provide a default executor, or users might be able to implement their own for specific needs.

The executor would be responsible for polling asynchronous operations (e.g., I/O, timers) and resuming the corresponding `async` functions when they are ready to make progress.

3. Integration with I/O and Timers:

The `async/await` feature will likely integrate with Zig's I/O and timer APIs in the standard library, allowing for non-blocking operations.

For example, you might be able to `await` the result of a non-blocking read from a socket or the completion of a timer.

4. Error Handling:

Error handling with `async`/`await` will likely integrate with Zig's existing error union (`!T`) mechanism. `async` functions might return `!Result`, and `await`ing a future that resolves to an error would propagate that error.

Potential Benefits of `async`/`await` **in Zig:**

Improved Concurrency without Heavy Threading: `async`/`await` allows for concurrent execution of many tasks without the overhead of creating and managing a large number of OS threads.

More Readable Asynchronous Code: It can make asynchronous code look more like synchronous code, improving readability and reducing the complexity of callback-based approaches.

Better Performance for I/O-Bound Tasks: For applications that involve a lot of waiting for I/O operations (network requests, file reads), `async`/`await` can lead to significant performance improvements by allowing the program to work on other tasks while waiting.

Current State and How to Stay Updated:

Experimental Stage: As of now, `async`/`await` in Zig is primarily in the experimental or proposal stage. You might find experimental implementations or discussions on the Zig issue tracker and community forums.

No Stable Release: Do not rely on `async`/`await` for production code yet, as the syntax and behavior are subject to change.

Follow Zig Development: To stay updated on the progress of `async`/`await` and other language features, follow the official Zig website (https://ziglang.org/), the Zig issue tracker on GitHub, and the Zig community channels (e.g., Discord, IRC).

In summary, while Zig doesn't currently have stable `async` and `await` keywords like some other languages, it is a highly anticipated feature under active development. When it becomes available, it will likely provide a more ergonomic and efficient way to achieve asynchronicity in Zig applications, especially for I/O-bound workloads. For now, concurrency in Zig is primarily achieved through the explicit use of threads and synchronization primitives. Keep an eye on the official Zig development channels for updates on the `async`/`await` feature.

6.3 Best Practices for Concurrent and Asynchronous Programming in Zig

Alright, let's discuss best practices for concurrent and asynchronous programming in Zig, keeping in mind that Zig's concurrency model primarily revolves around threads with explicit synchronization, and the `async`/`await` feature is under development but not yet stable.

Best Practices for Thread-Based Concurrency (Current Zig):

1.Minimize Shared Mutable State:

The more shared mutable state you have between threads, the more complex your synchronization logic becomes and the higher the risk of race conditions and deadlocks.

Strive to design your concurrent tasks to be as independent as possible.

When sharing state is necessary, carefully control access using synchronization primitives.

2. **Use Appropriate Synchronization Primitives:**

Atomic Operations (`std.atomic`**):** For simple counters, flags, or other basic types where you need thread-safe updates, prefer atomic operations as they are often more efficient than mutexes.

Mutexes (`std.Mutex`**):** Use mutexes to protect critical sections of code that access shared mutable data. Ensure that you always acquire the lock before accessing the data and release it afterward (ideally using `defer mutex.unlock()`).

Condition Variables (`std.Condition`**):** When a thread needs to wait for a specific condition to become true (often related to shared state protected by a mutex), use condition variables in conjunction with mutexes.

Reader-Writer Locks (`std.RwMutex` **- if available in your Zig version or a library):** If you have data that is read frequently but written infrequently, a reader-writer lock can allow multiple readers to access the data concurrently while ensuring exclusive access for writers.

3. **Be Mindful of Deadlocks:**

Deadlocks occur when two or more threads are blocked indefinitely, waiting for each other to release resources.[1]

Avoid Nested Locks: If possible, avoid acquiring multiple locks simultaneously. If you must, try to acquire them in a consistent order across all threads.

Use Timeouts (Carefully): Some synchronization primitives might offer timeout mechanisms. However, relying heavily on timeouts for correctness can be brittle. They are often better suited for detecting potential deadlocks or preventing indefinite blocking in certain scenarios.

4. Manage Thread Lifecycles Properly:

Join Threads: If the main thread needs to wait for worker threads to complete before exiting or continuing, use `thread.join()`. Failing to join threads can lead to data loss or unexpected program termination.

Consider Detached Threads (Carefully): In some cases, you might want to create detached threads that run independently of the main thread. However, be very careful with the lifecycle and resource management of detached threads, as the main thread won't wait for them.

5. Handle Errors in Threads:

Ensure that errors within worker threads are properly handled (e.g., logging, signaling the main thread if necessary). Unhandled panics in threads can lead to program termination.

Consider using channels (implemented manually or via a library) to send error information back to the main thread or other interested threads.

6. **Use Thread-Local Storage** (`std.Thread.LocalStorage`) **for Thread-Specific Data:**

If a piece of data is only relevant to a specific thread and doesn't need to be shared, use thread-local storage to avoid the need for synchronization.

7. **Design for Scalability:**

Consider how your concurrent design will scale with an increasing number of threads or tasks. Excessive thread creation can lead to context switching overhead. Thread pools (if you use a library) can help manage this.

Best Practices for Asynchronous Programming (Anticipating async/await**):**

While async/await is not yet stable, we can anticipate some best practices based on how it works in other languages and the likely design in Zig:

1.**Keep** async **Functions Short and Focused:**

Break down complex asynchronous operations into smaller, composable `async` functions to improve readability and maintainability.

2. Avoid Blocking Operations in `async` Functions:

The key to efficient asynchronicity is to avoid performing long-running synchronous (blocking) operations within `async` functions. If you need to perform blocking I/O or CPU-bound tasks, offload them to a separate thread pool and `await` the result.

3. Handle Errors in `async` Operations:

Use Zig's error union (`!T`) consistently with `async` functions and `await` expressions to ensure that errors are properly propagated and handled.

4. Be Aware of Potential for Deadlocks (with `async`/`await`):

While less common than in thread-based concurrency with explicit locks, deadlocks can still occur in asynchronous code, especially if you are waiting on a chain of tasks that depend on each other in a circular way within the same executor.

5. Choose the Right Executor:

Depending on your application's needs (e.g., I/O-bound vs. CPU-bound), you might need to choose or configure an appropriate executor for running your asynchronous tasks.

6. Cancellation of Asynchronous Tasks:

Implement mechanisms to cancel long-running asynchronous operations if they are no longer needed. This might involve using cancellation tokens or similar patterns.

7. Resource Management in Asynchronous Contexts:

Ensure that resources (e.g., file handles, network connections) are properly closed or released even if an asynchronous operation is cancelled or encounters an error. Use `defer` appropriately.

General Best Practices for Both Concurrency Models:

Keep it Simple: Concurrency and asynchronicity can introduce significant complexity. Strive for the simplest design that meets your requirements.

Thorough Testing: Write comprehensive tests that specifically target concurrent and asynchronous scenarios, including error handling and edge cases. Use tools like the testing allocator to detect memory leaks in concurrent contexts.

Profiling and Benchmarking: Use profiling tools to identify performance bottlenecks in your concurrent or asynchronous code and benchmark different approaches to find the most efficient solution.

Code Reviews: Have your concurrent and asynchronous code reviewed by others to catch potential issues related to synchronization, deadlocks, and race conditions.

Document Your Design: Clearly document the concurrency model you are using, how shared state is managed, and any synchronization strategies employed.

By following these best practices, you can write more robust, efficient, and maintainable concurrent and asynchronous Zig applications, whether you are using threads or leveraging the upcoming `async`/`await` features. Remember that explicitness and careful consideration of potential issues are key in Zig's low-level environment.

CHAPTER 7

Interoperability with C: Leveraging Existing Libraries

7.1 Understanding Zig's Seamless C Interoperability

Alright, let's explore Zig's renowned seamless C interoperability. This is one of Zig's standout features, allowing you to work with C codebases with minimal friction and significant advantages over traditional approaches.

Key Aspects of Zig's C Interoperability:

1.Direct Inclusion of C Headers:

Zig can directly parse and understand C header files (`.h`).[1] You can import C headers using `@cImport` within a `extern "c"` block.[2]

Zig's compiler acts as a full C99 preprocessor and parser, meaning it handles macros, includes, and other preprocessor directives.

2. Code snippet

```
const c = @cImport({
    @cInclude("stdio.h");
    @cInclude("stdlib.h");
});
```

```
pub fn main() !void {
    c.printf("Hello from Zig!\n");
    const random_number = c.rand();
    c.printf("Random number: %d\n", .{random_number});
}
```
3.

In this example, @cInclude brings in the declarations from stdio.h and stdlib.h, making functions like printf and rand directly accessible through the c namespace.

4. **Automatic Translation of C Types:**

Zig automatically translates C types to their corresponding Zig equivalents. For example:

int in C typically maps to c_int in Zig.

unsigned char* in C maps to [*c]u8 in Zig.

struct foo in C maps to c.foo in Zig.

This translation aims to be semantically equivalent, respecting size and alignment where possible. Zig provides explicit C-compatible integer types (e.g., c_int, c_uint, c_long) to ensure clarity when interacting with C code.[3]

5. **Direct Calling of C Functions:**

Once C headers are imported, you can directly call C functions as if they were native Zig functions through the c namespace (or whatever name you assign to the @cImport block).[4]

6. **Accessing C Data Structures:**

You can create and manipulate instances of C structs and unions directly in Zig. Zig respects the layout and padding of C data structures.[5]

7. Code snippet

```
const c = @cImport({
    @cInclude("stdint.h");

    typedef struct {
        uint32_t id;
        uint8_t name[64];
    } User;
});

pub fn main() !void {
    var user: c.User = .{
        .id = 123,
        .name = "ZigUser".*, // Use .* to convert Zig string to C array
```

```
    };

    c.printf("User ID: %u, Name: %s\n", .{user.id, &user.name});
}
```
8.

Note the use of .* to convert a Zig string literal to a null-terminated C-style array when initializing the name field.

9. Passing Zig Data to C Functions:

Zig allows you to pass Zig data structures and values to C functions, with appropriate care for type compatibility and memory layout.

Zig slices can often be passed to C functions expecting pointers and lengths.

10. Code snippet

```
const c = @cImport({
    @cInclude("stdio.h");
});

export fn printZigString(zig_string: []const u8) void {
    c.printf("Received from Zig: %s\n", .{zig_string.ptr});
}

pub fn main() !void {
    const message = "Hello C from Zig!";
```

```
    printZigString(message);
}
11.
```

Here, a Zig slice `[]const u8` is passed to a C function expecting a `const char*`. Zig automatically handles the pointer conversion.

12. Memory Management Across the Boundary:

Zig Manages Zig Memory: Memory allocated using Zig's allocators must be freed using the same allocator within Zig.

C Manages C Memory: Memory allocated by C functions (e.g., using `malloc`) must be freed by C functions (e.g., using `free`).[6] Zig does not automatically track or manage memory allocated by C. You need to be mindful of ownership and ensure proper allocation and deallocation on the C side.

Passing Pointers: When passing pointers between Zig and C, be aware of which side owns the memory and is responsible for freeing it.

13. `extern "c"` Blocks:

The `@cImport` directive must reside within an `extern "c"` block. This tells the Zig compiler that the imported declarations and any Zig functions declared within this block should adhere to the C calling convention, ensuring compatibility with C code.

14. Building C Libraries with Zig:

Zig can also be used to build C libraries.[7] You can write Zig code and expose a C API that can be consumed by C programs.

Advantages of Zig's C Interoperability:

Minimal Overhead: Zig's C interop is designed to be low-overhead.[8] There's no separate foreign function interface (FFI) layer that introduces significant runtime costs.

Safety: Zig's strong typing and compile-time checks extend to the C interop layer, helping to catch potential type mismatches and errors at compile time rather than runtime.

Ease of Use: The direct inclusion of headers and automatic type translation make it remarkably easy to work with C code without writing extensive wrapper code.

Cross-Compilation: Zig's excellent cross-compilation capabilities extend to C interop. You can often cross-compile projects that depend on C libraries with relative ease.

Gradual Adoption: You can start using Zig in an existing C project incrementally, leveraging Zig for new modules or performance-critical sections while still benefiting from existing C libraries.[9]

Potential Challenges:

Memory Management Responsibility: The manual nature of memory management becomes even more critical when crossing the Zig-C boundary. You need to be very careful about who owns the memory.

Error Handling Differences: C's error handling mechanisms (e.g., return codes, `errno`) are different from Zig's error unions. You might need to write some bridging code to handle errors effectively across the boundary.

Complex C Macros: While Zig's preprocessor is capable, very complex or unusual C macros might require some manual adaptation or workarounds.

In summary, Zig's C interoperability is a powerful and well-designed feature that allows developers to leverage the vast ecosystem of C libraries with a high degree of safety and ease. It's a key reason why Zig is attractive for systems programming, embedded development, and projects that need to interact with existing C codebases.

7.2 Importing and Utilizing C Libraries in Your Zig Projects

Alright, let's walk through the process of importing and utilizing C libraries within your Zig projects. This will build upon the understanding of Zig's seamless C interoperability we just discussed.

Steps to Import and Utilize a C Library:

1.Identify the C Library and its Headers:

First, you need to know the C library you want to use and have access to its header files (`.h`). These files contain the declarations of functions, structs, constants, etc., that you'll need to interact with.

You might need to install the C library and its development headers on your system (e.g., using `apt-get install` `libxyz-dev` on Debian/Ubuntu or a similar package manager on other systems).

2. **Create a `build.zig` File (if you don't have one):**

If you're building a more complex project, you'll likely have a `build.zig` file that defines how your Zig project is built. For simple examples, you can often directly use a `.zig` source file and compile it. However, for linking against external C libraries, `build.zig` is generally necessary.

3. Code snippet

```
const std = @import("std");
const Builder = std.build.Builder;

pub fn build(b: *Builder) !void {
    const target = b.standardTargetOptions(.{});
    const optimize = b.standardOptimizeOption(.{});

    const exe = b.addExecutable(.{
        .name = "myzigapp",
        .root_source_file = .{ .path = "src/main.zig" },
        .target = target,
        .optimize = optimize,
    });

    // Step 3: Link against the C library
    exe.linkLibC(); // For standard C library functions (often needed)
        exe.linkSystemLibrary("mylclibrary"); // Replace "mylclibrary"
with the actual name
```

```
    b.installArtifact(exe);
}
```
4.

In this `build.zig` example:

`exe.linkLibC()` links against the system's standard C library.

`exe.linkSystemLibrary("mylclibrary")` tells the Zig build system to link against a system library named "mylclibrary" (e.g., `libmylclibrary.so` or `mylclibrary.lib`). You'll need to replace `"mylclibrary"` with the actual name of the library you want to use.

5. Import the C Headers in Your Zig Code:

In your Zig source file (e.g., `src/main.zig`), use `@cImport` within an `extern "c"` block to include the necessary C header files.

6. Code snippet


```
const c = @cImport({
    @cInclude("stdio.h");
    @cInclude("mylclibrary.h"); // Replace with the actual header file
});
```

```zig
pub fn main() !void {
    c.printf("Hello from Zig using stdio!\n");

    // Now you can call functions and access definitions from
    "mylclibrary.h"
    const result = c.some_function_from_mylclibrary(123);
    c.printf("Result from my C library: %d\n", .{result});

    // ... use other functions and data structures from the C library ...
}
```
7.

Replace `"mylclibrary.h"` with the actual header file provided by the C library. If the header file is not in a standard include path, you might need to provide additional include paths to `@cImport` (see the advanced options below).

8. **Build and Run Your Zig Project:**

Use the Zig build command to compile and link your project:

9. Bash

```bash
zig build run
```
10.

The Zig build system will take care of finding the C library (assuming it's installed in a standard location or you've provided the necessary paths) and linking it with your Zig executable.

Advanced Options for `@cImport`:

The `@cImport` directive accepts a struct literal with various options to control how C headers are processed:

`.includes = &[_][]const u8{"/usr/local/include",` `"./include"}`: Specifies an array of include directories to search for header files. This is useful if the C library's headers are not in the standard system include paths.

`.link_directories = &[_][]const u8{"/usr/local/lib", "./lib"}`: Specifies an array of library directories to search for the compiled C library.

`.link_libc = true`: Links against the system's standard C library (equivalent to `exe.linkLibC()` in `build.zig`).

`.link_system_libraries = &[_][]const u8{"mylclibrary", "anotherlib"}`: Links against system libraries (equivalent to `exe.linkSystemLibrary()` in `build.zig`).

`.define = &[_][]const u8{"MY_MACRO=1", "DEBUG"}`: Defines preprocessor macros.

`.undefine = &[_][]const u8{"MY_OLD_MACRO"}`: Undefines preprocessor macros.

`.flags = &[_][]const u8{"-Wall", "-O2"}`: Passes additional compiler flags to the C compiler.

Example with Advanced `@cImport` **Options:**

Code snippet

```
const c = @cImport({
    .includes = &[_][]const u8{"/opt/mylclibrary/include"},
    .link_directories = &[_][]const u8{"/opt/mylclibrary/lib"},
    .link_system_libraries = &[_][]const u8{"mylclibrary"},
    .define = &[_][]const u8{"USE_FEATURE_X"},
    @cInclude("mylclibrary.h");
    @cInclude("stdio.h");
});

pub fn main() !void {
    c.printf("Using my custom C library!\n");
    const result = c.some_function_from_mylclibrary(456);
    c.printf("Result: %d\n", .{result});
}
```

In this case, the `build.zig` might be simpler as the library linking information is provided within `@cImport`:

Code snippet

```
const std = @import("std");
const Builder = std.build.Builder;

pub fn build(b: *Builder) !void {
    const target = b.standardTargetOptions(.{});
    const optimize = b.standardOptimizeOption(.{});

    const exe = b.addExecutable(.{
        .name = "myzigapp",
        .root_source_file = .{ .path = "src/main.zig" },
        .target = target,
        .optimize = optimize,
    });
```

```
    b.installArtifact(exe);
}
```

Choosing Between `build.zig` and `@cImport` for Linking:

For simpler projects or when the C library is very standard (like `libc`), you might be able to handle linking primarily within the `@cImport` options.

For more complex projects with multiple dependencies or custom build steps, managing linking in `build.zig` is generally cleaner and more organized. It separates the concerns of defining the executable and its dependencies.

Important Considerations:

Memory Management: Remember that Zig doesn't automatically manage memory allocated by C functions. You'll need to call the appropriate C `free()` function (or its equivalent) from Zig when you're done with memory allocated by C.

Error Handling: C libraries typically use return codes or global variables like `errno` to indicate errors. You'll need to check these values in your Zig code after calling C functions and translate them into Zig's error union mechanism if you want consistent error handling.

String Handling: C strings are null-terminated `char` arrays. When passing Zig strings (`[]const u8`) to C functions expecting `char*`, you might need to ensure null termination. Similarly, when receiving strings from C, you'll need to handle the null terminator appropriately to create a valid Zig string.

Build Dependencies: Ensure that the C library you're trying to use is available in your build environment (installed on the system or provided in a specific location).

By following these steps and understanding the nuances of Zig's C interoperability, you can effectively import and utilize a wide range of C libraries in your Zig projects, leveraging existing C code while benefiting from Zig's safety and performance features.

7.3 Best Practices for Bridging Zig and C Codebases

Alright, bridging Zig and C codebases effectively requires careful consideration of several factors to ensure safety, maintainability, and performance. Here are some best practices to guide you:

1. Define Clear Boundaries and Interfaces:

Isolate C Code: Encapsulate your C code within specific modules or files in your Zig project. This makes it easier to manage the C dependencies and reason about the interactions.

Design Stable C APIs: If you're writing C code to be consumed by Zig, aim for a stable and well-defined C API. Minimize changes to this API to avoid breaking Zig code.

Create Zig Abstractions: Consider creating Zig wrappers or abstractions over the raw C API to provide a more idiomatic and safer Zig interface. This can involve handling memory management, error translation, and data structure conversions.

2. Manage Memory Explicitly and Carefully:

Know Ownership: Clearly define which side (Zig or C) is responsible for allocating and freeing memory. Document this ownership.

Zig Frees Zig Memory, C Frees C Memory: Never try to free memory allocated by C using Zig's allocators, and vice versa. Use the corresponding allocation and deallocation functions on each side.

Passing Memory: When passing pointers across the boundary, be extremely careful about lifetimes and ownership. Ensure that the memory remains valid for the duration it's being used by the other side. Consider using opaque pointers (`*opaque`) in Zig to represent C data structures when Zig doesn't need to know the internal layout, limiting direct manipulation and potential for errors.

Use `defer` for Zig-Allocated Memory: If Zig allocates memory that's passed to C, use `defer allocator.free()` to ensure it's freed when no longer needed in Zig.

3. Handle Errors Gracefully Across the Boundary:

Translate C Errors to Zig Errors: C often uses return codes (e.g., `-1` on error, `errno`) to signal failures. In your Zig wrappers, check these return codes and translate them into Zig's error union (`!T`) mechanism for consistent error handling.

Consider Returning Optionals for Nullable Pointers: If a C function can return a `NULL` pointer to indicate failure or an absent value, consider returning an optional type (`?*C.struct_t`) in your Zig wrapper.

Document C Error Handling: Clearly document how errors are reported by the C functions you are using and how you are handling them in Zig.

4. Manage Strings Carefully:

Null Termination for C: When passing Zig strings (`[ ]const u8`) to C functions expecting `char*`, ensure they are null-terminated if the C function expects a C-style string. You might need to allocate a temporary buffer with a null terminator.

Zig Slices for C Arrays: For passing fixed-size C arrays to Zig, you can often use Zig slices with a known length.

Creating Zig Strings from C Strings: When receiving `char*` from C, determine the length of the C string (e.g., using `c.strlen`) and create a Zig slice from the pointer and length. Be mindful of the encoding (UTF-8 is often a good default in Zig).

5. Respect Calling Conventions and Types:

`extern "c"` **Blocks:** Always enclose your `@cImport` and Zig function declarations that interact with C within `extern "c"` blocks to ensure C calling conventions are used.

Use Corresponding Types: Be mindful of the type translations between C and Zig (e.g., `int` to `c_int`). Use the appropriate Zig C-compatible types to avoid unexpected behavior due to size or representation differences. Explicit casts (`@intCast`, `@ptrCast`) can be necessary but use them with caution and understanding.

6. Build System Integration:

`build.zig` **Configuration:** Use `build.zig` to properly link against the C libraries. Specify include paths, library paths, and library names correctly.

Conditional Compilation: If your Zig code needs to interact with different C libraries or versions, use conditional compilation (`@if`, `@hasFeature`) based on build options or target platforms.

7. Testing Across the Boundary:

Write Integration Tests: Create tests that specifically exercise the interaction between your Zig and C code. Test both successful scenarios and error conditions.

Memory Leak Detection: Pay close attention to memory management in your tests to ensure you're not leaking memory on either the Zig or C side. Tools like Valgrind can be invaluable for this.

8. Documentation and Comments:

Document C Dependencies: Clearly document which C libraries your Zig project depends on and how they are being used.

Comment Interop Code: Add comments to explain the purpose and intricacies of the code that bridges Zig and C, especially around memory management, error handling, and type conversions.

9. Consider Alternatives (When Appropriate):

Pure Zig Implementations: Before relying heavily on C libraries, consider if there are mature and performant pure Zig alternatives available or if implementing the functionality in Zig offers advantages in terms of safety and maintainability.

Higher-Level Bindings: For some popular C libraries, the Zig community might have created higher-level, more idiomatic Zig bindings that handle many of the interop complexities for you. Explore these options before writing your own low-level bindings.

10. Stay Updated with Zig's Development:

Zig's C interoperability is a key feature, and the language and standard library might evolve. Stay informed about the latest recommendations and best practices from the Zig community.

By following these best practices, you can create robust and maintainable bridges between your Zig and C codebases, leveraging the strengths of both languages while minimizing potential pitfalls. The key is to be explicit, careful with memory management, and to handle errors and data conversions thoughtfully.

CHAPTER 8

Testing and Debugging: Ensuring Reliability and Performance

8.1 Writing Effective Unit Tests and Integration Tests in Zig

Alright, let's dive into writing effective unit tests and integration tests in Zig. As we discussed, Zig's built-in `std.testing` provides a solid foundation for this.

1. Unit Tests:

Unit tests focus on verifying the correctness of individual, isolated units of code, such as functions, methods, or small modules. The goal is to ensure that each piece of your code works as expected in isolation.

Best Practices for Effective Unit Tests:

Test One Thing at a Time: Each unit test should focus on verifying a single aspect or behavior of the unit under test. This makes it easier to pinpoint the source of a failure.

Arrange, Act, Assert (AAA): Structure your tests following the AAA pattern:

Arrange: Set up the necessary preconditions, inputs, and dependencies for the test.

Act: Execute the specific piece of code you are testing.

Assert: Verify that the actual output or side effects match the expected outcome using `std.debug.assert`.

Code snippet

```
const std = @import("std");
const assert = std.debug.assert;

fn multiply(a: i32, b: i32) i32 {
    return a * b;
}

test "multiply positive numbers" {
    // Arrange
    const x = 5;
    const y = 3;
    const expected = 15;

    // Act
    const actual = multiply(x, y);

    // Assert
    assert(actual == expected);
}
```

Test Boundary Conditions and Edge Cases: Think about the extreme or unusual inputs your code might receive (e.g., zero, negative numbers, empty strings, maximum/minimum values). These often reveal subtle bugs.

Code snippet

```
test "multiply with zero" {
    assert(multiply(10, 0) == 0);
    assert(multiply(0, -5) == 0);
}

test "multiply with negative numbers" {
    assert(multiply(-2, 4) == -8);
    assert(multiply(-3, -3) == 9);
}
```

Test Error Conditions: If your function can return errors (using error unions), write tests to ensure that it returns the correct errors under the expected circumstances. Use `catch` to handle the expected errors in your tests.

Code snippet

```
const std = @import("std");
const assert = std.debug.assert;
const testing = std.testing;

const DivisionError = error { DivideByZero };

fn safeDivide(a: i32, b: i32) !i32 {
    if (b == 0) {
        return DivisionError.DivideByZero;
```

```
    }
    return a / b;
}

test "safeDivide by non-zero" {
    try assert(safeDivide(10, 2) == 5);
}

test "safeDivide by zero returns error" {
    const result = safeDivide(5, 0);
    assert(result == DivisionError.DivideByZero);
}

test "safeDivide by zero using catch" {
    const result = safeDivide(1, 0) catch |err| err;
    assert(result == DivisionError.DivideByZero);
}
```

Use Mocking/Stubbing for Dependencies (Carefully): When a unit under test relies on external dependencies (e.g., file system, network), it can be helpful to replace these dependencies with controlled test doubles (mocks or stubs) to isolate the unit's behavior. Zig doesn't have a built-in mocking framework, so you might need to create these manually using interfaces or function pointers. However, be cautious not to over-mock, as this can lead to tests that don't accurately reflect real-world behavior.

Keep Tests Fast and Isolated: Unit tests should be quick to run and should not have external side effects that can interfere with other tests. Each test should be able to run independently.

Write Tests That Fail Clearly: When an assertion fails, the error message should provide enough information to understand what went wrong. Use descriptive test names and assertion messages if necessary.

Test for Memory Leaks: If the unit under test allocates memory, use `std.testing.allocator` to ensure that all allocated memory is freed within the test.

Code snippet

```
test "function with memory allocation frees it" {
    var test_allocator = testing.allocator;
    {
        const buffer = try allocateBuffer(test_allocator.allocator(), 10);
        defer test_allocator.allocator().free(buffer);
        // ... use buffer ...
    }
    try test_allocator.expectLeaks();
}
```

2. Integration Tests:

Integration tests focus on verifying the interactions between different parts or modules of your system. They ensure that these components work together correctly.

Best Practices for Effective Integration Tests:

Test Interactions Between Components: Focus on how different modules or services communicate and collaborate to achieve a higher-level functionality.

Test Realistic Scenarios: Design integration tests to mimic real-world use cases of your application.

Set Up Realistic Environments (if feasible): Depending on the complexity of your system, you might need to set up simplified versions of external dependencies (e.g., a lightweight in-memory database or a mock network service) for your integration tests.

Test Across Layers: Integration tests might span multiple layers of your application (e.g., testing the interaction between the business logic layer and the data access layer).

Consider End-to-End Tests: For larger systems, end-to-end tests (a type of integration test) simulate the entire user flow, interacting with the application as a user would.

Manage Test Data and State: Carefully manage the data used in your integration tests to ensure consistency and avoid test pollution. You might need to set up a clean state before each test and tear it down afterward.

Integration Tests Can Be Slower: Integration tests often involve more setup and interaction with external systems, so they might take longer to run than unit tests. It's important to strike a balance between thoroughness and execution time.

Focus on Key Integrations: Prioritize testing the most critical integrations in your system.

Organizing Tests in Zig:

Same File: You can define tests directly within the same `.zig` file as the code they are testing. This can be convenient for smaller units.

Separate `test.zig` Files: For larger projects, it's often better to create separate files (e.g., `my_module_test.zig`) in a `test/` directory that import and test the corresponding source files. This helps keep your source code cleaner and makes it easier to find tests.

`build.zig` **Integration:** The `build.zig` file automatically discovers and runs tests in your project when you use the `zig build test` command. You don't typically need to do extra configuration to include your test files.

Example of Separate Test File (`test/math_test.zig`):

Code snippet

```
const std = @import("std");
const assert = std.debug.assert;
const math = @import("../src/math.zig"); // Assuming math.zig is in
the src directory

test "math.add works" {
    assert(math.add(2, 3) == 5);
    assert(math.add(-1, 1) == 0);
}

test "math.subtract works" {
    assert(math.subtract(5, 2) == 3);
    assert(math.subtract(0, 5) == -5);
```

}

Corresponding Source File (`src/math.zig`):

Code snippet

```
pub fn add(a: i32, b: i32) i32 {
    return a + b;
}

pub fn subtract(a: i32, b: i32) i32 {
    return a - b;
}
```

By following these guidelines, you can write effective unit and integration tests in Zig that help ensure the reliability and correctness of your software. Remember that a good testing strategy involves a mix of both types of tests, with a greater emphasis on fast and isolated unit tests.

8.2 Utilizing Zig's Built-in Testing Framework and Tools

Alright, let's dive deeper into utilizing Zig's built-in testing framework and tools (`std.testing`). We've touched on the basics, but there's more to explore to help you write effective and comprehensive tests.

1. Test Discovery and Execution:

Automatic Discovery: When you run `zig test` or `zig build test`, the Zig build system automatically discovers all functions in your project that are annotated with the `test` keyword. You don't need to manually list test files or functions.

Running Specific Tests (Future): While not a fully mature feature as of my last update, Zig's test runner is evolving and might gain the ability to run specific tests by name or file in the future. Keep an eye on the Zig documentation for updates on this.

Test Output: The test runner provides clear output indicating which tests passed and which failed, along with any assertion failure messages and stack traces (in debug builds).

2. Advanced Assertions and Utilities:

`std.testing.expectEqual` **and Similar:** The `std.testing` module might offer more specific assertion functions beyond `std.debug.assert` for common comparison scenarios (e.g., floating-point equality with tolerance). Check the `std.testing` module documentation for the latest offerings.

Code snippet

```
const std = @import("std");
const testing = std.testing;

test "floating point equality with tolerance" {
    const a: f32 = 1.000001;
    const b: f32 = 1.000002;
    testing.expectEqual(a, b, 0.00001); // Might exist in std.testing
}
```

Expect Errors: You can write tests that specifically expect a function to return a particular error. This ensures your error handling logic is working correctly.

Code snippet

```
test "function returns expected error" {
    const result = tryOpenFile("non_existent.txt") catch |err| err;
        testing.expectError(std.fs.Error.FileNotFound, result); // Might
exist in std.testing
}

fn tryOpenFile(path: []const u8) !std.fs.File {
    return std.fs.openFile(path, .{});
}
```

Skipping Tests (Future): The ability to mark tests as skipped might be added to the testing framework in the future for cases where a test is known to be failing or is not yet ready to be run.

3. Test Fixtures and Setup/Teardown:

For tests that require setting up and tearing down resources (e.g., creating temporary files, initializing data structures), you might need to implement setup and teardown logic within each test function. Zig doesn't have explicit @BeforeEach or @AfterEach annotations like some other frameworks, but you can achieve similar behavior with defer.

Code snippet

```
const std = @import("std");
const testing = std.testing;
const fs = std.fs;

test "file operation with setup and teardown" {
    var file: ?fs.File = null;
    const tmp_file_path = "test_temp.txt";

    // Setup
    const result = fs.openFile(tmp_file_path, .{}).?;
    file = result;
    defer if (file) |f| f.close();
    const content = "Test data";
    try file.?.writeAll(content);

    // Act
    const read_content = try fs.readFileAlloc(testing.allocator,
tmp_file_path);
    defer testing.allocator.free(read_content);

    // Assert
    testing.expectEqualStrings(content, read_content); // Might exist
in std.testing

    // Teardown (using defer) - file will be closed and memory freed
    try fs.deleteFile(tmp_file_path);
}
```

For more complex setup that needs to happen once per test file, you might use a global variable and initialize it within a `test` block that runs first. However, be cautious with global mutable state in tests.

4. Integration with the Build System (`build.zig`):

`b.addTest`: In your `build.zig` file, you can explicitly add test executables using `b.addTest`. This can be useful for more complex test setups or when you want to separate integration tests into different executables.

Code snippet

```
const std = @import("std");
const Builder = std.build.Builder;

pub fn build(b: *Builder) !void {
    const target = b.standardTargetOptions(.{});
    const optimize = b.standardOptimizeOption(.{});

    const exe = b.addExecutable(.{
        .name = "myzigapp",
        .root_source_file = .{ .path = "src/main.zig" },
        .target = target,
        .optimize = optimize,
    });
    b.installArtifact(exe);

    // Add a test executable
    const test_exe = b.addTest(.{
        .name = "myzigapp_tests",
        .root_source_file = .{ .path = "test/main.zig" },
        .target = target,
        .optimize = optimize,
    });

    // Define a build step to run the tests
    const run_tests = b.step("test", "Run all tests");
```

```
    run_tests.dependOn(test_exe.step);
}
```

In this `build.zig`, we define a separate test executable that runs the tests in `test/main.zig`. The `test` build step depends on the successful completion of this test executable.

Dependencies in Tests: Your test code can import and use the modules you are testing, ensuring that the tests are tightly coupled with the code they verify.

5. Best Practices for Testability:

Design for Testability: Write code that is easy to test. This often means breaking down complex logic into smaller, well-defined functions with clear inputs and outputs.

Reduce Global State: Global mutable state can make testing harder because tests might interfere with each other. Prefer passing dependencies explicitly.

Dependency Injection: Consider using dependency injection (passing dependencies as arguments) to make it easier to replace real dependencies with test doubles in your tests.

Clear Separation of Concerns: Modules and functions with a single responsibility are generally easier to test.

6. Continuous Integration (CI):

Zig's straightforward build system and test runner make it easy to integrate Zig projects with CI/CD pipelines. You can typically run `zig build test` in your CI environment to automatically execute your tests on every commit or pull request.

In summary, Zig's built-in testing framework provides a clean and efficient way to write and run tests. By leveraging the `test` keyword, `std.debug.assert` (and potentially more specialized assertions in `std.testing`), the test allocator for memory leak detection, and by structuring your tests well, you can ensure the reliability of your Zig applications. Integrating tests with the build system makes it easy to automate testing as part of your development process.

8.3 Advanced Debugging Techniques for High-Performance Zig Applications

Alright, let's delve into advanced debugging techniques specifically tailored for high-performance Zig applications. When performance is critical, traditional step-by-step debugging can be too slow or might even alter the behavior you're trying to observe. Here are some more sophisticated approaches:

1. Profiling and Performance Analysis:

Built-in Profiler (Experimental): As mentioned earlier, Zig has an experimental built-in profiler. Learn how to use it to collect timing information about different parts of your code. This can pinpoint performance bottlenecks far more effectively than stepping through line by line. Focus your debugging efforts on the functions that consume the most execution time.

System Profilers (e.g., `perf` on Linux, Instruments on macOS): Integrate with system-level profiling tools. These tools can provide a broader view of your application's resource usage (CPU, memory, cache behavior) and can sometimes offer insights that language-specific profilers might miss. You can often record profiling data while running your application under realistic workloads.

Flame Graphs: Visualize profiling data using flame graphs. These graphs provide a clear representation of the call stack and the amount of time spent in each function, making it easier to identify hot paths. Tools like `perf` can often generate data that can be converted into flame graphs using external utilities.

2. Logging and Tracing:

Structured Logging: Implement a robust logging system that records relevant information about your application's state and execution flow. Use structured logging (e.g., JSON format) to make it easier to search, filter, and analyze logs, especially in high-throughput scenarios. Include timestamps, thread IDs (if applicable), and contextual information.

Tracing: For understanding the sequence of events and the timing of operations across different parts of your application, consider using tracing. Libraries or custom implementations can record the start and end times of significant events, allowing you to visualize the flow and identify latency issues. Tools like Jaeger or Zipkin (though you might need to build Zig integrations) can be powerful for distributed tracing.

Conditional Logging: Implement different logging levels (e.g., debug, info, warn, error) and configure your application to output more detailed logs only when needed for debugging specific issues or during development. This avoids overwhelming logs in production.

3. Statistical Sampling and Observability:

Sampling: Instead of tracing every single operation, consider statistical sampling, where you only collect detailed information for a small percentage of requests or events. This can significantly reduce the overhead of debugging in high-load systems while still providing valuable insights into overall behavior.

Metrics and Monitoring: Integrate your application with metrics collection systems (e.g., Prometheus) to expose key performance indicators (KPIs) like request latency, throughput, error rates, and resource utilization. Monitoring these metrics in real-time can help you identify performance regressions or anomalies.

Alerting: Set up alerts based on your metrics to be notified automatically when performance degrades beyond acceptable thresholds. This allows you to proactively investigate issues.

4. Specialized Debugging Tools and Techniques:

Memory Profiling: Use memory profiling tools (if available for Zig or through OS-level tools) to understand how your application is allocating and using memory. This can help identify memory leaks, excessive allocation, or fragmentation issues that can impact performance. Tools like Valgrind (with its massif tool) can be helpful, though you might need to run your application in a controlled environment.

Cache Analysis Tools: If cache performance is critical, explore tools that can help you analyze cache hits and misses (e.g., `perf` with cache-related events). Understanding cache behavior can be crucial for optimizing data access patterns in high-performance applications.

Concurrency-Specific Debugging:

Thread Analyzers: Tools like ThreadSanitizer (often part of the Clang toolchain and potentially usable with Zig-compiled code) can help detect data races and other concurrency-related issues that can lead to unpredictable behavior and performance problems.

Visualizations: For complex concurrent systems, consider using visualization tools to understand thread interactions, lock contention, and message passing (if you're using channels or similar constructs).

Hardware Performance Counters: Utilize hardware performance counters (accessed through tools like `perf`) to get low-level insights into CPU cycles, instructions retired, cache misses, branch mispredictions, etc. This can be invaluable for fine-tuning performance-critical sections of code.

5. Controlled Experiments and Benchmarking:

Isolate Performance-Critical Sections: Identify the parts of your code that are most performance-sensitive and create isolated benchmarks for them using `std.testing.benchmark`.

A/B Testing and Canary Deployments: When making performance-related changes, consider using A/B testing or canary deployments in a staging or production-like environment to compare the performance of the new version against the old version under real load.

Microbenchmarking with Care: While microbenchmarks can be useful for comparing small code snippets, be cautious about extrapolating these results to the overall application performance. Real-world workloads are often more complex and can introduce different bottlenecks.

6. Debug Builds vs. Release Builds:

Understand Optimization Effects: Be aware that compiler optimizations in release builds can significantly alter the execution flow and make traditional step-by-step debugging more challenging. The behavior you observe in a debug build might not be exactly the same as in a release build.

Debug in Release (Carefully): Sometimes, performance issues only manifest in release builds. You might need to debug release builds, but be prepared for the optimized code to be less straightforward to step through. Consider using logging and profiling more heavily in these scenarios.

`-Doptimize=Debug`: Use the `-Doptimize=Debug` build option to get a build with some optimizations but still retaining debugging information. This can be a good middle ground for investigating performance-related bugs.

Key Principles for Advanced Debugging:

Understand Your System: Have a deep understanding of your application's architecture, its dependencies, and the expected performance characteristics.

Reproduce the Issue: Try to reproduce the performance problem in a controlled environment where you can apply your debugging techniques.

Measure, Don't Guess: Rely on data from profiling and monitoring tools rather than making assumptions about where the bottlenecks are.

Iterate and Validate: Make small, targeted changes based on your analysis and then re-measure to verify the impact of your changes.

Document Your Findings: Keep track of the debugging steps you've taken, the data you've collected, and the conclusions you've reached.

By mastering these advanced debugging techniques, you can effectively diagnose and resolve performance issues in your high-performance Zig applications, ensuring they meet your requirements for speed and efficiency. Remember to leverage the right tools for the specific problem you are trying to solve.

CHAPTER 9

Optimizing Zig Applications: Achieving Peak Performance

9.1 Profiling and Benchmarking Zig Code: Identifying Bottlenecks

Alright, let's dive deep into profiling and benchmarking Zig code to effectively identify performance bottlenecks in your applications. Zig provides built-in tools and integrates well with system profilers to help you gain insights into your code's performance.

1. Benchmarking with `std.testing.benchmark`:

Zig's built-in testing framework allows you to write benchmark functions to measure the execution time of specific code snippets.

Defining Benchmarks: Use the `benchmark` keyword followed by a descriptive name and a block of code that you want to measure. The benchmark function receives a `*BenchmarkContext` which provides utilities for controlling the benchmark.

Code snippet

```
const std = @import("std");
const testing = std.testing;
const time = std.time;

fn slowFunction(n: u32) u64 {
    var result: u64 = 0;
    for (0..n) |i| {
        result += @as(u64, i) * i;
```

```
    }
    return result;
}

benchmark "slowFunction with n=1000" {
    const n: u32 = 1000;
    _ = slowFunction(n);
}

benchmark "fastFunction with n=1000" {
    const n: u32 = 1000;
    var result: u64 = 0;
    var i: u32 = 0;
    while (i < n) : (i += 1) {
        result += @as(u64, i) * i;
    }
    _ = result;
}

benchmark "allocate and free 1MB" {
    var            arena            =
std.heap.ArenaAllocator.init(testing.allocator.allocator());
    defer arena.deinit();
    const allocator = arena.allocator();
    const size: usize = 1024 * 1024;
    const buffer = try allocator.alloc(u8, size);
    defer allocator.free(buffer);
}
```

Running Benchmarks: Use the `zig build bench` command in your terminal. Zig will execute all `benchmark` functions in your project and report the average execution time per iteration.

Bash

```
zig build bench
# ... output ...
benchmark slowFunction with n=1000... 1000 iterations in
0.00502s (5.02us/iter)
benchmark fastFunction with n=1000... 1000 iterations in 0.00251s
(2.51us/iter)
benchmark allocate and free 1MB... 1000 iterations in 0.00015s
(0.15us/iter)
```

Benchmark Context (`*BenchmarkContext`): The `BenchmarkContext` (though not explicitly used in the simple examples above) provides more control over the benchmark execution, such as setting the number of iterations or performing setup and teardown. Refer to the `std.testing` documentation for advanced usage.

2. Profiling with System Tools:

Zig executables can be profiled using standard operating system profiling tools. This gives you a system-wide view of your application's performance.

Linux (perf): perf is a powerful command-line profiling tool for Linux.[1]

1.Build your Zig application (ideally with debug info for better symbol resolution):

2. Bash

zig build -Doptimize=ReleaseFast your_program.zig
3.

4. Run your application under perf:

5. Bash

sudo perf record -F 99 -p $(pidof your_program) -g -- call-graph dwarf,65536
# or, to profile the entire execution:
sudo perf record -F 99 -g ./zig-out/bin/your_program
6.

7. `-F 99`: Sample at 99Hz (samples per second). `-p $(pidof your_program)`: Profile a running process. `-g --call-graph dwarf,65536`: Record call graph information using DWARF debugging symbols.

8. Analyze the recorded data:

9. Bash

```
perf report -g
# or to generate a flame graph (requires additional tools like 'FlameGraph' repository):
perf script | stackcollapse-perf.pl | flamegraph.pl > flamegraph.svg
10.
```

macOS (`Instruments`): Instruments is a graphical performance analysis tool bundled with Xcode.

11. Build your Zig application (with debug symbols):

12. Bash

```
zig build -Doptimize=ReleaseFast your_program.zig
```

13.

14. Open Instruments: Launch Instruments from Xcode or Spotlight.[2]

15. Choose a profiling template: The "Time Profiler" is often a good starting point.

16. Select your Zig executable: Attach to your running Zig process or select the executable to launch with Instruments.

17. Start recording: Run your application and perform the actions you want to profile.

18. Analyze the results: Instruments provides detailed information about CPU usage, call stacks, and more. You can identify the functions where your application spends the most time.

Windows (`perfmon`, `xperf`): Windows provides Performance Monitor (`perfmon`) and the Windows Performance Toolkit (WPT), which includes `xperf`.

19. Build your Zig application.

20. Use `perfmon`: Search for "Performance Monitor" in the Start Menu. You can add counters to track CPU usage, memory, and other metrics for your Zig process.

21. Use `xperf` **(more advanced):**

Start tracing: `xperf -start PerfDiag -on PROC_THREAD+LOADER+DISK_IO+NETWORK`

Run your application.

Stop tracing: `xperf -stop PerfDiag -d trace.etl`

Analyze the trace: Open `trace.etl` with Windows Performance Analyzer (WPA), which is part of the Windows Performance Toolkit.[3]

3. Identifying Bottlenecks:

Once you have benchmark data or profiling information, you can start identifying bottlenecks:

High CPU Usage: If your profiler shows high CPU usage in specific functions, those are potential bottlenecks. Examine the code within those functions for inefficient algorithms, unnecessary computations, or excessive looping.

Memory Allocation: Frequent or large memory allocations can be expensive. Use benchmarking to measure the cost of allocation and profiling to see where allocations occur. Consider using arena allocators or other memory management strategies to reduce overhead.

I/O Operations: Disk I/O, network requests, and other I/O-bound operations can be significant bottlenecks. Use profiling to see how much time your application spends waiting for I/O. Consider asynchronous operations (when `async/await` becomes stable) or optimizing I/O patterns.

Synchronization Primitives: In concurrent applications, excessive lock contention or inefficient use of synchronization primitives (mutexes, atomics) can lead to bottlenecks.[4] Profiling can show where threads are spending time waiting.

Algorithm Complexity: Ensure that you are using algorithms with appropriate time and space complexity for your data sizes and workloads. A seemingly small inefficiency in an algorithm can become a major bottleneck with large inputs.

Cache Misses: High cache miss rates can significantly impact performance. System profilers can sometimes provide information about cache behavior.[5] Optimize data access patterns to improve cache locality.

External Libraries/System Calls: If your Zig code interacts heavily with C libraries or makes many system calls, profile these interactions to see if they are contributing to bottlenecks.

Best Practices for Profiling and Benchmarking:

Benchmark Realistic Scenarios: Design benchmarks that closely resemble how your application will be used in the real world.

Run Benchmarks Multiple Times: Get an average execution time by running benchmarks multiple times to account for variations in system load.

Profile Under Load: Profile your application under realistic workloads to identify bottlenecks that might only appear under pressure.

Compare Different Implementations: Benchmark different algorithms or approaches to solve the same problem to find the most efficient one.

Focus on the Hotspots: Don't try to optimize everything at once. Concentrate your efforts on the parts of the code that profiling reveals as the most time-consuming.

Measure Before and After Optimization: Always benchmark or profile your code before and after making changes to ensure that your optimizations are actually having the desired effect.

Use Release Builds for Performance Analysis: Always profile and benchmark release builds (`-Doptimize=ReleaseFast` or similar) as debug builds can have significant performance overhead.

Isolate Benchmarks: Ensure that your benchmark environment is as isolated as possible to minimize interference from other processes.

By effectively utilizing Zig's built-in benchmarking capabilities and integrating with system profiling tools, you can gain valuable insights into your application's performance and identify the bottlenecks that need optimization. Remember that a data-driven approach is crucial for successful performance tuning.

9.2 Low-Level Optimization Techniques: SIMD, Data Layout, and More

Alright, let's delve into the realm of low-level optimization techniques in Zig, focusing on SIMD, data layout, and other strategies that can significantly boost the performance of your applications when fine-grained control is necessary.

1. Single Instruction, Multiple Data (SIMD):

SIMD allows you to perform the same operation on multiple data elements simultaneously using specialized processor instructions. This can lead to massive speedups for data-parallel tasks.

Zig's SIMD Support (`std.simd`): Zig provides the `std.simd` module, which offers types and functions for working with SIMD vectors. The level of SIMD support available depends on the target architecture.

Code snippet

```
const std = @import("std");
const simd = std.simd;
const assert = std.debug.assert;

test "add two SIMD vectors of i32" {
    if (simd.Scalar(i32).is_native) {
        const a = simd.Vector(4, i32).init(1, 2, 3, 4);
        const b = simd.Vector(4, i32).init(5, 6, 7, 8);
```

```zig
        const result = a + b;
        assert(result[0] == 6);
        assert(result[1] == 8);
        assert(result[2] == 10);
        assert(result[3] == 12);
    } else {
        std.debug.warn("SIMD for i32 (vector of 4) is not native on this target.\n", .{});
    }
}


fn scalarMultiply(vector: simd.Vector(4, f32), scalar: f32) simd.Vector(4, f32) {
    return vector * simd.Vector(4, f32).splat(scalar);
}

test "scalar multiply SIMD vector of f32" {
    if (simd.Scalar(f32).is_native) {
        const v = simd.Vector(4, f32).init(1.0, 2.0, 3.0, 4.0);
        const s: f32 = 2.5;
        const result = scalarMultiply(v, s);
        assert(result[0] == 2.5);
        assert(result[1] == 5.0);
        assert(result[2] == 7.5);
        assert(result[3] == 10.0);
    } else {
        std.debug.warn("SIMD for f32 (vector of 4) is not native on this target.\n", .{});
    }
}
```

Checking for SIMD Support: Use `simd.Scalar(T).is_native` to check if SIMD operations are natively supported for a given scalar type T and vector size on the target architecture. This allows you to provide fallback implementations for targets without SIMD.

Vector Types: `simd.Vector(N, T)` represents a SIMD vector with N elements of type T.

Operations: Standard arithmetic operators (+, -, *, /) are overloaded for SIMD vectors, performing element-wise operations.

`splat`: The `splat` method creates a SIMD vector where all elements have the same scalar value.

Loading and Storing Data: You'll often need to load data from memory into SIMD vectors and store results back. The `std.mem.load` and `std.mem.store` functions, along with pointer casting, can be used for this, but be mindful of alignment requirements for optimal SIMD performance.

Horizontal Operations: SIMD also often provides horizontal operations (e.g., summing all elements in a vector), which can be useful for reducing the results of parallel computations. Check the `std.simd` module for available horizontal operations.

2. Data Layout Optimization:

How you arrange your data in memory can have a significant impact on performance due to cache locality and SIMD vectorization.

Structure of Arrays (SoA) vs. Array of Structures (AoS):

AoS: Stores data for each entity contiguously in memory (e.g., `[{x: f32, y: f32}, {x: f32, y: f32}, ...]`). This is often natural but can be less efficient for SIMD operations that want to operate on all `x` coordinates together, then all `y` coordinates.

SoA: Stores data for different attributes of multiple entities in separate arrays (e.g., `xs: [f32]`, `ys: [f32]`). This layout is often more SIMD-friendly as you can load contiguous blocks of the same attribute into SIMD vectors.

Code snippet

```
// Array of Structures (AoS)
const PointAoS = struct { x: f32, y: f32 };
const points_aos = [_]PointAoS{{ .x = 1, .y = 2 }, { .x = 3, .y = 4 }, {
.x = 5, .y = 6 }};

// Structure of Arrays (SoA)
const PointsSoA = struct { xs: [3]f32, ys: [3]f32 };
const points_soa = PointsSoA{ .xs = .{1, 3, 5}, .ys = .{2, 4, 6} };
```

Choose the data layout that best suits how your data is processed, especially if you're using SIMD.

Padding and Alignment: Ensure that your data structures are aligned correctly for the target architecture and for optimal SIMD vector loads and stores. Zig respects alignment requirements. Be aware of potential padding added by the compiler, which can sometimes affect SIMD performance if not considered. You can use `@alignOf` and `@sizeOf` to inspect the layout of your data structures.

Cache Locality: Arrange data that is accessed together close together in memory to improve cache hits. Consider the order in which data is accessed and how you can structure your data to exploit spatial locality.

3. Other Low-Level Optimization Techniques:

Loop Unrolling: For small, predictable loops, the compiler might automatically unroll them to reduce loop overhead and potentially expose more instruction-level parallelism. You can sometimes influence this with compiler flags or by manually unrolling loops (though this can reduce code readability).

Instruction Selection: While Zig gives you more control than some higher-level languages, the compiler still ultimately selects the specific machine instructions. Understanding the target architecture's instruction set can sometimes help you write code that the compiler can translate into more efficient instructions. However, focus on higher-level optimizations first.

Branch Prediction: Minimize unpredictable branches in performance-critical code, as branch mispredictions can stall the CPU pipeline. Techniques like branchless programming (using conditional moves or bitwise operations instead of `if` statements) can sometimes help, but they can also reduce readability. Profile to see if branching is a significant bottleneck.

Function Inlining: The compiler can inline small, frequently called functions to reduce function call overhead. You can use the `inline` keyword (though it's just a hint to the compiler) to suggest inlining.

Custom Memory Allocation: For specific use cases, the default allocator might not be the most performant. Consider using custom allocators (e.g., arena allocators for bulk allocation/deallocation, pool allocators for fixed-size objects) to reduce allocation overhead and improve memory locality.

Pointer Aliasing: Be mindful of pointer aliasing, where multiple pointers might refer to the same memory location. This can sometimes hinder compiler optimizations. Using Zig's strict aliasing rules can help the compiler generate more efficient code.

Builtins: Zig provides built-in functions (@) that give you direct access to certain low-level operations. Use these judiciously when you need fine-grained control (e.g., `@bitCast`, `@intCast`, `@alignOf`).

Assembly (`asm`): As a last resort, Zig allows you to embed assembly code directly within your Zig functions using the `asm` keyword. This gives you the ultimate control over the generated instructions but sacrifices portability and can be harder to maintain. Use assembly only when absolutely necessary and when you have a deep understanding of the target architecture.

Best Practices for Low-Level Optimization:

Profile First: Always identify the bottlenecks in your code through profiling before attempting low-level optimizations. Premature optimization can be a waste of time and might even make your code slower or harder to maintain.

Measure the Impact: After applying any optimization, benchmark your code to quantify the performance improvement. Ensure that your changes actually made a difference.

Prioritize Readability and Maintainability: Low-level optimizations can sometimes make code harder to read and understand. Balance performance gains with maintainability. Add comments to explain any non-obvious optimizations.

Target Specific Architectures: SIMD and other low-level features are often architecture-dependent. Be aware of the target architectures you are optimizing for and potentially provide different code paths for different targets.

Iterate and Refine: Low-level optimization is often an iterative process. You might need to try different techniques and measure their impact to find the best solution.

By understanding and applying these low-level optimization techniques in Zig, you can achieve significant performance improvements in your applications when the default compiler optimizations are not sufficient. Remember to always profile and benchmark to guide your optimization efforts.

9.3 Cross-Compilation and Platform-Specific Optimizations

Alright, let's explore the crucial aspects of cross-compilation and platform-specific optimizations in Zig. These are vital for ensuring your applications run efficiently and correctly across a variety of target platforms.

1. Cross-Compilation in Zig:

Zig's build system has first-class support for cross-compilation, making it remarkably easy to build your code for different operating systems and architectures from a single development environment.

Target Specification: You specify the target platform using the `-target` command-line option with `zig build` or by configuring it in your `build.zig` file. Targets are defined by a triple consisting of the architecture, operating system, and ABI (Application Binary Interface).

Bash

```
# Cross-compile for 64-bit Linux (GNU ABI on glibc)
zig build -target x86_64-linux-gnu

# Cross-compile for 32-bit Windows (MSVC ABI)
zig build -target i386-windows-msvc

# Cross-compile for ARM64 macOS
zig build -target aarch64-macos-none
```

`build.zig` **Configuration:** You can configure the target within your `build.zig` file using the `target` field in the `addExecutable` or `addLibrary` calls. You can also use the `b.standardTargetOptions(.{})` helper to get the target specified by the user during the build invocation.

Code snippet

```zig
const std = @import("std");
const Builder = std.build.Builder;

pub fn build(b: *Builder) !void {
    const target = b.standardTargetOptions(.{});
    const optimize = b.standardOptimizeOption(.{});

    const exe = b.addExecutable(.{
        .name = "myzigapp",
        .root_source_file = .{ .path = "src/main.zig" },
        .target = target, // Use the target specified by the user
        .optimize = optimize,
    });

    b.installArtifact(exe);
}
```

Standard Library for Different Targets: Zig's standard library is designed to be cross-platform. When you cross-compile, the appropriate parts of the standard library for the target platform are used. However, some platform-specific functionality might only be available on certain targets.

C Interoperability in Cross-Compilation: Zig's seamless C interop extends to cross-compilation. You can often include C headers and link against C libraries for your target platform, provided you have the necessary toolchain (e.g., cross-compiling GCC or Clang) and target libraries available. Zig handles much of the complexity of finding the right headers and libraries.

2. Platform-Specific Optimizations:

To achieve optimal performance on different platforms, you might need to apply platform-specific optimizations. Zig provides mechanisms to detect the target platform at compile time and apply different code paths or optimization strategies.

`@target` **Builtin:** The `@target` builtin provides information about the target architecture, operating system, and ABI during compilation. You can use this within `@if` or `comptime` blocks to conditionally execute code based on the target.

Code snippet

```
const std = @import("std");

pub fn main() !void {
    std.debug.print("Target: {}\n", .{@target()});

    comptime {
        if (@target().os == .linux) {
            std.debug.print("Running on Linux.\n", .{});
            // Apply Linux-specific optimizations
        } else if (@target().os == .windows) {
            std.debug.print("Running on Windows.\n", .{});
            // Apply Windows-specific optimizations
        } else if (@target().arch == .x86_64) {
            std.debug.print("Running on x86_64 architecture.\n", .{});
            // Apply x86_64-specific optimizations (e.g., SIMD)
        }
    }

    // Runtime checks if needed
    if (@import("builtin").os == .linux) {
```

```
    // ...
  }
}
```

Feature Detection: Zig might provide builtins or standard library functions to detect specific CPU features (e.g., AVX-512 support). You can use this information to enable or disable certain optimizations at runtime or compile time. Check the `std.cpu` module if available.

Conditional Compilation in `build.zig`: You can also use the target information in your `build.zig` file to configure build options or link against platform-specific libraries.

Code snippet

```
const std = @import("std");
const Builder = std.build.Builder;

pub fn build(b: *Builder) !void {
    const target = b.standardTargetOptions(.{});
    const optimize = b.standardOptimizeOption(.{});

    const exe = b.addExecutable(.{
        .name = "myzigapp",
        .root_source_file = .{ .path = "src/main.zig" },
        .target = target,
        .optimize = optimize,
    });
```

```
    if (target.os == .linux) {
        exe.linkSystemLibrary("rt"); // Link against the real-time library
on Linux
    } else if (target.os == .windows) {
        exe.linkSystemLibrary("ws2_32"); // Link against Winsock on
Windows
    }

    if (target.arch == .x86_64) {
        exe.addCDefine("ARCH_X86_64", "1");
    } else if (target.arch == .aarch64) {
        exe.addCDefine("ARCH_AARCH64", "1");
    }

    b.installArtifact(exe);
}
```

Platform-Specific Standard Library Usage: Be aware that some parts of the standard library might have platform-specific implementations that are optimized for the underlying operating system or architecture.

Examples of Platform-Specific Optimizations:

SIMD Intrinsics: Using `@target` to detect the architecture (e.g., `x86_64`) and then using platform-specific SIMD intrinsics (if Zig provides direct access or through C interop with compiler intrinsics) for vectorized computations.

Memory Allocation Strategies: Choosing different memory allocation strategies based on the target platform's memory management characteristics.

Concurrency Primitives: Utilizing platform-specific concurrency primitives (e.g., Windows fibers vs. POSIX threads) if they offer performance advantages for certain workloads, though Zig's standard library aims to provide portable abstractions.

System Calls: For very low-level optimizations, you might consider making direct system calls, but this severely reduces portability. Zig's standard library usually provides safer and more portable abstractions.

Assembly Code: As a last resort, you can use inline assembly (asm) that is specific to the target architecture, but this should be done with extreme caution and only when necessary.

Best Practices for Cross-Compilation and Platform-Specific Optimizations:

Prioritize Portability: Aim for a single codebase that works well across multiple platforms. Apply platform-specific optimizations only when necessary to achieve significant performance gains on specific targets.

Abstract Platform Differences: When you do need platform-specific code, try to abstract it behind a common interface to minimize the impact on the rest of your codebase.

Test Thoroughly on Each Target: Always test your application thoroughly on all target platforms you intend to support to ensure correctness and that your optimizations are working as expected.

Use Feature Detection Over OS/Architecture Checks: Where possible, detect specific CPU features rather than relying solely on the operating system or architecture, as features can vary within the same architecture.

Document Platform-Specific Code: Clearly document any platform-specific optimizations and the reasons behind them.

Consider Build Flags: Allow users to control which optimizations are enabled at build time through options in your `build.zig`.

Profile on Target Hardware: Always profile your application on the actual target hardware to get accurate performance measurements. Emulators can sometimes give misleading results.

Zig's excellent cross-compilation support and its ability to detect the target platform at compile time provide a powerful foundation for building high-performance applications that can be tailored to specific environments. By using these features judiciously, you can achieve the best possible performance across your supported platforms.

CHAPTER 10

Advanced Topics and Real-World Applications of Zig

10.1 Metaprogramming with Zig: Compile-Time Reflection and Code Generation

Alright, let's explore the fascinating world of metaprogramming in Zig, focusing on its powerful compile-time reflection and code generation capabilities. Zig's approach to metaprogramming is deeply integrated with its type system and compile-time execution, offering a unique and efficient way to generate code and introspect types.

1. Compile-Time Reflection with `@typeInfo`:

Zig provides the `@typeInfo` builtin function, which allows you to inspect the type of any Zig value or type at compile time. This is the foundation of Zig's reflection capabilities.

Basic Type Information: `@typeInfo` returns a structure containing detailed information about the given type, such as its kind (e.g., `Int`, `Float`, `Struct`, Enum, `Array`, `Pointer`), size, alignment, fields (for structs), cases (for enums), and more.

Code snippet

```
const std = @import("std");

const MyStruct = struct {
    id: u32,
    name: [32]u8,
```

```zig
};

const MyEnum = enum {
    A,
    B,
    C,
};

pub fn main() !void {
    comptime var struct_info = @typeInfo(MyStruct);
    std.debug.print("Struct Kind: {}\n", .{struct_info.kind});
    std.debug.print("Struct Name: {s}\n", .{@typeName(MyStruct)});
    std.debug.print("Struct Field Count: {}\n", .{struct_info.Struct.fields.len});
    for (struct_info.Struct.fields) |field| {
        std.debug.print("  Field Name: {s}, Type: {s}\n", .{field.name, @typeName(field.type)});
    }

    comptime var enum_info = @typeInfo(MyEnum);
    std.debug.print("Enum Kind: {}\n", .{enum_info.kind});
    std.debug.print("Enum Name: {s}\n", .{@typeName(MyEnum)});
    std.debug.print("Enum Case Count: {}\n", .{enum_info.Enum.cases.len});
    for (enum_info.Enum.cases) |case| {
        std.debug.print("  Case Name: {s}, Value: {}\n", .{case.name, case.value});
    }
}
```

Accessing Type-Specific Information: The result of `@typeInfo` is a tagged union. You need to switch on the `kind` field to access the type-specific information within the corresponding union member (e.g., `struct_info.Struct`, `enum_info.Enum`).

`@typeName`: The `@typeName` builtin returns a `[]const u8` representing the name of a given type at compile time, which is useful for generating human-readable output or code.

2. Compile-Time Code Generation with `comptime` and Loops:

Zig's `comptime` keyword allows you to execute arbitrary Zig code at compile time. Combined with loops and conditional statements, this enables powerful code generation based on type information or other compile-time constants.

Generating Code Based on Struct Fields: You can iterate over the fields of a struct using `@typeInfo` within a `comptime` block and generate code for each field.

Code snippet

```
const std = @import("std");

const MyData = struct {
    id: u32,
    value: f32,
    name: [16]u8,
};

fn printField(comptime field: @TypeOf(.{ .name = "", .type = i32 }))
void {
```

```
        std.debug.print("Field Name: {s}, Type: {s}\n", .{field.name,
@typeName(field.type)});
    }

pub fn main() !void {
    comptime var info = @typeInfo(MyData).Struct.fields;
    comptime {
        for (info) |field| {
            printField(field); // 'field' is comptime here
        }
    }
}
```

Generating Data Structures or Functions: You can use `comptime` loops to generate multiple similar data structures or functions based on a set of compile-time parameters.

Code snippet

```
const std = @import("std");

comptime {
    for ([_]i32{1, 2, 4}) |power| {
        const ArrayType = [power]i32;
                std.debug.print("Generated Array Type: {s}\n",
.{@typeName(ArrayType)});
    }
}

comptime {
```

```
for ([_]struct { name: []const u8, value: i32 }{
    .{ .name = "add_five", .value = 5 },
    .{ .name = "add_ten", .value = 10 },
}) |op| {
    const FnType = fn (i32) i32;
    const generated_fn: FnType = comptime fn (x: i32) i32 {
        return x + op.value;
    };
    std.debug.print("Generated function {s}(3) = {}\n", .{op.name,
generated_fn(3)});
  }
}
```

3. Compile-Time Function Execution:

Any Zig function can be executed at compile time if all its arguments are comptime-known. This allows you to perform complex computations at compile time and use the results to generate code or data structures.

Code snippet

```
const std = @import("std");

comptime fn generateLookupTable(size: usize) [size]f32 {
    var table: [size]f32 = undefined;
    for (0..size) |i| {
        table[i] = @sin(@as(f32, @floatFromInt(i) /
@floatFromInt(size) * std.math.pi * 2));
    }
    return table;
}
```

```zig
comptime const sin_table = generateLookupTable(256);

pub fn main() !void {
    std.debug.print("Sine table value at index 10: {}\n",
.{sin_table[10]});
}
```

4. Metaprogramming for Serialization, Reflection, and More:

Zig's metaprogramming capabilities are incredibly useful for tasks like:

Automatic Serialization/Deserialization: You can generate code to serialize and deserialize data structures to various formats (e.g., JSON, binary) by inspecting their fields at compile time.

Automatic Field Iteration and Processing: Generate code to iterate over and process the fields of arbitrary structs, as shown in the `printField` example.

Code Generation for Interfacing with External Data Formats: Generate code to read and write data in specific file formats or network protocols based on their structure.

Implementing Generic Data Structures and Algorithms: While Zig doesn't have traditional generics, you can use comptime parameters and code generation to create data structures and algorithms that work with different types.

Generating Boilerplate Code: Reduce repetitive code by generating it at compile time based on type information or other parameters.

5. Limitations and Considerations:

Compile-Time Errors: Errors in your `comptime` code will result in compile-time errors, which can sometimes be harder to debug than runtime errors.

Complexity: Overuse of metaprogramming can make your code harder to understand and maintain if not done carefully.

Performance Implications: While metaprogramming can improve runtime performance by generating specialized code, excessive compile-time computation can increase build times.

Best Practices for Metaprogramming in Zig:

Use `@typeInfo` Judiciously: Only use reflection when you need to operate on types in a generic way at compile time.

Keep `comptime` Code Focused: Make your compile-time code clear and focused on the code generation task.

Test Generated Code: Ensure that the code generated by your metaprogramming logic is thoroughly tested.

Consider Alternatives: Sometimes, runtime polymorphism or other language features (if applicable) might be a simpler solution than complex metaprogramming.

Document Your Metaprogramming: Clearly document the purpose and logic of your metaprogramming code, as it can be less obvious than regular runtime code.

Zig's compile-time reflection and code generation provide a powerful toolkit for building flexible, efficient, and maintainable software. By leveraging `@typeInfo`, `comptime`, and compile-time function execution, you can automate code generation and create highly specialized solutions. However, it's important to use these features thoughtfully and balance their power with code clarity and maintainability.

10.2 Building Networked Applications and System Utilities with Zig

Alright, let's explore building networked applications and system utilities with Zig. Zig's strengths in low-level control, performance, and safety make it a compelling choice for both these domains.

1. Building Networked Applications with Zig:

Zig's standard library (`std.net`) provides the fundamental building blocks for creating various types of networked applications.

Sockets: The `std.net.Socket` type allows you to work with TCP and UDP sockets. You can create, bind, listen (for TCP servers), connect (for TCP clients), send, and receive data.

Code snippet

```
const std = @import("std");
const log = std.debug.print;
const net = std.net;
const time = std.time;

// Simple TCP Echo Server
fn runTcpServer() !void {
    const listener = try net.tcp.listen(net.Address.ipv4(std.net.ip.Address.loopback, 8080));
    defer listener.close();
    log("TCP Echo Server listening on port 8080...\n", .{});
```

```
  while (true) {
    const client = try listener.accept();
    std.thread.spawn(.{}, handleTcpClient, client) catch |err| {
      log("Error spawning client handler: {}\n", .{err});
      client.close();
    };
  }
}

fn handleTcpClient(client: net.tcp.Connection) !void {
  defer client.close();
  var buf: [1024]u8 = undefined;
  while (true) {
    const len = try client.read(&buf);
    if (len == 0) break; // Connection closed by client
    try client.writeAll(buf[0..len]); // Echo back
  }
  log("TCP Client disconnected.\n", .{});
}

// Simple UDP Sender
fn runUdpSender() !void {
  const socket = try net.udp.open(net.AddressFamily.ipv4);
  defer socket.close();
    const addr = net.Address.ipv4(std.net.ip.Address.loopback,
9000);
  const msg = "Hello UDP!";
  try socket.send(addr, msg);
  log("UDP message sent to {}:{}: {}\n", .{addr.ip, addr.port, msg});
}

pub fn main() !void {
    if (std.os.argv.len > 1 and std.mem.eql(u8, std.os.argv[1],
"server")) {
```

```
    try runTcpServer();
  } else if (std.os.argv.len > 1 and std.mem.eql(u8, std.os.argv[1],
"udp")) {
    try runUdpSender();
  } else {
    log("Usage: {} [server|udp]\n", .{std.os.argv[0]});
  }
}
```

HTTP and TLS (Community Libraries): While the standard library provides core networking primitives, higher-level protocols like HTTP and secure communication via TLS/SSL are typically handled by community-maintained libraries. Look for packages on Zig's package manager (when it matures) or on platforms like GitHub.

Asynchronous Networking (Future async/await**):** The upcoming async/await feature in Zig will significantly enhance the ability to write efficient, non-blocking networked applications without the complexities of manual thread management.

JSON and Serialization (Standard Library): The std.json module in the standard library is excellent for handling JSON data, which is commonly used in networked applications. You can parse and serialize JSON efficiently.

Concurrency for Networked Applications: Zig's thread support (std.Thread) allows you to handle multiple network connections concurrently, as demonstrated in the TCP server example.

2. Building System Utilities with Zig:

Zig's low-level capabilities and direct access to system APIs make it well-suited for creating system utilities.

File System Operations (`std.fs`): The `std.fs` module provides comprehensive functions for interacting with the file system: creating, opening, reading, writing, deleting files and directories, getting file metadata, etc.

Code snippet

```
const std = @import("std");
const fs = std.fs;
const log = std.debug.print;

fn readFile(path: []const u8) ![]u8 {
    const file = try fs.openFile(path, .{});
    defer file.close();
    return try file.readToEndAlloc(std.heap.page_allocator);
}

fn writeFile(path: []const u8, contents: []const u8) !void {
    const file = try fs.createFile(path, .{});
    defer file.close();
    try file.writeAll(contents);
}

pub fn main() !void {
    if (std.os.argv.len == 3 and std.mem.eql(u8, std.os.argv[1], "read")) {
        const contents = try readFile(std.os.argv[2]);
        log("Contents of {s}:\n{s}\n", .{std.os.argv[2], contents});
        std.heap.page_allocator.free(contents);
```

```
    } else if (std.os.argv.len == 4 and std.mem.eql(u8,
std.os.argv[1], "write")) {
    try writeFile(std.os.argv[2], std.os.argv[3]);
    log("Wrote '{s}' to {s}\n", .{std.os.argv[3], std.os.argv[2]});
  } else {
      log("Usage: {} [read <path> | write <path> <contents>]\n",
.{std.os.argv[0]});
  }
}
```

Operating System Interaction (`std.os`): The `std.os` module provides functions for interacting with the operating system: getting command-line arguments, environment variables, process management, signals, etc.

Command-Line Argument Parsing (`std.Args`): The `std.Args` struct helps in parsing command-line arguments provided to your utility.

Concurrency for Utilities: For utilities that perform parallel operations (e.g., processing multiple files), Zig's threads can be used to improve performance.

Low-Level System Access: Zig allows you to perform low-level system operations when needed, including interacting with hardware (though this might require platform-specific code and careful use of pointers).

Cross-Compilation for Utilities: You can easily cross-compile your system utilities for different target platforms using Zig's build system.

Advantages of Zig for Networked Applications and System Utilities:

Performance: Zig's focus on performance and low-level control allows you to build highly efficient networked applications and system utilities.

Safety: Zig's memory safety features help prevent common bugs like buffer overflows and dangling pointers, which are crucial in both networking and system programming.

Small Binaries and No Runtime Dependencies: Zig compiles to small, self-contained executables without external runtime dependencies (like a large virtual machine), making deployment easier for both network services and command-line utilities.

Concurrency Primitives: Zig's built-in thread support enables you to build concurrent applications that can handle multiple network connections or parallel processing tasks efficiently.

Standard Library: The standard library provides essential tools for networking, file system operations, and OS interaction.

Cross-Compilation: Zig's excellent cross-compilation capabilities make it easy to target multiple platforms.

C Interoperability: You can leverage existing C libraries for networking (e.g., `libuv`, `openssl`) or system-level tasks if needed.

Challenges:

Ecosystem Maturity: Zig's ecosystem is still growing. Higher-level libraries for specific networking protocols or advanced system utilities might not be as readily available as in more mature languages.

Manual Memory Management: While Zig's safety features help, you still need to manage memory explicitly, which can be more complex than in garbage-collected languages.

Conclusion:

Zig is a promising language for building both networked applications and system utilities. Its performance, safety features, standard library, and cross-compilation capabilities provide a strong foundation. As the ecosystem matures, we can expect even more powerful tools and libraries to emerge, making Zig an increasingly attractive choice for these domains. For now, be prepared to potentially build some higher-level abstractions yourself or rely on community efforts.

10.3 Case Studies: Professional Projects Leveraging the Power of Zig

Alright, let's explore some case studies of professional projects that are leveraging the power of Zig. While Zig is still a relatively young language, it's gaining traction in various domains where its unique combination of performance, safety, and low-level control is highly valued.[1] Keep in mind that the ecosystem is still evolving, so many projects might be in earlier stages or might not be widely publicized yet. However, here are some examples and areas where Zig is making a mark:

1. Systems Programming and Infrastructure:

Mach kernel development (Hypershell): Hypershell is a modern terminal emulator built with Zig. It leverages Zig's performance for low latency and its safety features for a robust user experience. Developing a terminal emulator requires careful management of low-level system resources and handling asynchronous events efficiently, areas where Zig excels. This project showcases Zig's ability to build complex, performance-critical system tools.

Operating System Components (Redox OS): While Redox OS is primarily written in Rust, there are components and tools within the Redox ecosystem that are being explored or built with Zig for its low-level capabilities and simpler build process compared to C. This highlights Zig's potential in contributing to operating system development.

Embedded Systems and Firmware (Various projects): Zig's small binary sizes, lack of a large runtime, and direct memory management make it attractive for embedded systems and firmware development.[2] While specific large-scale professional deployments might not be widely public, there's growing interest and experimentation in using Zig for microcontrollers and embedded Linux systems. Its ability to cross-compile easily to various architectures is a significant advantage here.

2. Game Development:

Game Engines and Libraries (Mach engine, community efforts): The Mach engine, also from the Hypershell team, is an experimental game engine being built with Zig.[3] Game development often demands high performance for rendering and game logic, as well as careful memory management.[4] Zig's capabilities in these areas make it a promising language for building game engines and libraries. The community is also exploring Zig for various game development tools and libraries.

High-Performance Game Logic: Even if the core engine is in another language, Zig can be used to implement performance-critical parts of game logic as shared libraries due to its excellent C interoperability.[5] This allows game developers to benefit from Zig's speed and safety in specific areas.

3. WebAssembly (Wasm) and Frontend Development:

High-Performance Wasm Modules (Various projects): Zig's ability to compile to small and fast WebAssembly modules is a significant advantage. Projects requiring high-performance computations in the browser or other Wasm environments are exploring Zig. This includes areas like audio/video processing, scientific simulations, and complex web applications.[6]

Frontend Frameworks and Tools (Experimental): There are experimental efforts within the Zig community to build frontend frameworks or tools that leverage Zig's performance and Wasm capabilities. While not yet mainstream, this area shows potential for Zig in web development beyond just backend services.

4. Command-Line Tools and Utilities:

Modern Replacements for Core Utilities (e.g., `ls`, `cat`): Zig's speed and low dependencies make it an excellent choice for building fast and efficient command-line tools.[7] There are community projects aiming to create modern replacements for standard Unix utilities written in Zig. These tools benefit from Zig's performance and memory safety.

Developer Tools (Build systems, Linters): Zig's build system itself is written in Zig, showcasing its ability to create complex developer tools.[8] The community is also exploring using Zig for linters, formatters, and other tools where performance and correctness are crucial.

5. Networking and Distributed Systems:

High-Performance Network Services (Experimental): While the standard library networking is still evolving, Zig's performance characteristics make it suitable for building high-performance network services.[9] Projects requiring low latency and high throughput are likely to explore Zig as the networking ecosystem matures.

Distributed Systems Components: Zig's ability to compile to small, self-contained binaries could be beneficial for building components of distributed systems where resource efficiency and predictable behavior are important.

Challenges and Considerations:

Ecosystem Maturity: Zig's library ecosystem is still smaller compared to more established languages like Go, Rust, or C++. For complex projects, you might need to rely on C interoperability or contribute to building Zig libraries.

Learning Curve: While Zig aims for simplicity, its unique approach to memory management and error handling can have a learning curve for developers coming from other languages.

Production Readiness: For very large-scale, mission-critical projects, some organizations might still be cautious about adopting a relatively newer language like Zig. However, early adopters are demonstrating its potential.

How to Find More Case Studies:

Zig Community Forums and Chat Channels: Engage with the Zig community on platforms like Discord, IRC, and the official Zig forums.[10] Developers often share their projects and experiences there.

GitHub and GitLab: Search for Zig projects on these platforms. Look for actively developed projects with a significant number of stars and contributors.

Zig Conferences and Meetups: Keep an eye out for Zig-related conferences and meetups, where developers often present their work.

Official Zig Blog and Website: The official Zig website and blog might feature case studies or highlight projects in the future.

Conclusion:

While the list of large, widely publicized professional projects solely built with Zig might still be growing, the examples above and the increasing interest in the language demonstrate its potential in performance-critical domains. Zig's unique combination of features makes it a compelling choice for systems programming, game development, WebAssembly, command-line tools, and potentially networking and distributed systems as the ecosystem matures. Keep an eye on the Zig community and its growing adoption in various professional contexts.

www.ingramcontent.com/pod-product-compliance
Lightning Source LLC
LaVergne TN
LVHW012334060326
832902LV00012B/1883